JESUS

JESUS

A Biblical Defense
of His Deity

by
Josh McDowell
and
Bart Larson

CAMPUS CRUSADE FOR CHRIST
Published by
HERE'S LIFE PUBLISHERS, INC.
San Bernardino, California 92402

JESUS
A Biblical Defense of His Deity
by Josh McDowell
and Bart Larson

A Campus Crusade for Christ Book
Published by
HERE'S LIFE PUBLISHERS, INC.
P.O. Box 1576
San Bernardino, CA 92402

Library of Congress Catalog Card 83-071923
ISBN 0-86605-114-7
HLP Product No. 403212
© 1983 Here's Life Publishers, Inc.

Scripture quotations are from the New American Standard Bible, © The Lockman Foundation 1960, 1962, 1963, 1968, 1971, 1972, 1973, 1975, and are used by permission.

FOR MORE INFORMATION, WRITE:
L.I.F.E.—P.O. Box A399, Sydney South 2000, Australia
Campus Crusade for Christ of Canada—Box 368, Abbottsford, B.C., V25 4N9, Canada
Campus Crusade for Christ—103 Friar Street, Reading RGI IEP, Berkshire, England
Lay Institute for Evangelism—P.O. Box 8786, Auckland 3, New Zealand
Great Commission Movement of Nigeria—P.O. Box 500, Jos, Plateau State Nigeria, West Africa
Life Ministry—P.O. Box/Bus 91015, Auckland Park 2006, Republic of South Africa
Campus Crusade for Christ International—Arrowhead Springs, San Bernardino, CA 92414, U.S.A.

CONTENTS

Foreword

I initially examined Christianity in order to write a book making a mockery of it. I thought I would be dealing either with a theological ideology or with a philosophical proposition couched in theological terms. To me, Christianity was no more than a religion based on the teachings of its founder. There were simple religious principles to live by, a standard to live up to.

After extensive research, however, I discovered that Christianity is not a religion of men and women working their way to God through "good works." Nor is it obedience to a pattern of religious ritual. Rather, it is a relationship with a living God through His Son Jesus Christ. To my amazement, I was confronted with a *person,* not a religion. Here was a person who made staggering claims about Himself, along with profound claims on *my* life. Jesus was so different from what I had expected. Other religious leaders put their teachings out in front. Jesus put Himself out in front. Others would ask, "How are you responding to my teachings?" Jesus asked, "How are you related to *me*?"

My personal struggle had brought me face to face with a person—Jesus Christ. But was He who He claimed to be?

In other books (*Evidence That Demands a Verdict, More Than a Carpenter, The Resurrection Factor,* etc.) I have outlined some of the evidence, both biblical and historical, that has convinced me that Jesus is the Son of God. Since writing those other books, I've sensed a need for a book centering on the biblical claims of Jesus to be God in human flesh, God incarnate. Let Bart and me share our study and findings with you here.

Josh McDowell

Chapter 1

Jesus Christ Is God

If one were to ask a panel of religious experts of differing faiths what God is like and how God has revealed Himself, one could expect as many different opinions as there were panel members. The answers of some of them would contradict the answers of others. If we make the assumption that truth is not relative, they could not all be right. For example, if one says that God is personal and another that God is impersonal, then obviously one of them is wrong. Who can say for sure what God is like? The only One who can say *for sure* is God Himself.

So then, what if one of the panel members stood up and said, "To clear up all the confusion about God, I announce to you that I AM GOD! I am THE way, THE truth, and THE life!"?

This gets into the verifiable. Either this man is psychotic, with delusions of grandeur, or a deceiver out to pull off the greatest hoax of all time—or he is God.

That is the type of claim Jesus made for Himself. To say that Jesus was "just" a good moral man or a good teacher is out of the question. Good moral men don't make a practice of lying, either intentionally or unintentionally, especially about being God Almighty. They don't set themselves up as the object of faith and worship, and have countless thousands die for belief in their name. With these thoughts in mind, let us look at some ways we can determing the truth about God.

God Is Revealed

The present authors believe God has revealed Himself in various ways, but each of them can be objectively tested by His two supreme revelations, the Bible and the person of Jesus.

First, concerning the Bible. Unlike many other sacred writings the Bible claims unequivocally to be the Word of God. Most people concerned with the issue of Christ's divinity accept the Bible as inspired. So, for the purposes of this book, we are going to assume that the Bible is historically reliable, God's Word to us, and the one true guide for determining whether or not Christ is God incarnate.

Let us be very candid on why we feel this particular point is so important. The vast majority of religious groups which deny the deity of Christ, while giving lip service to the Bible, usually elevate other "sacred" writings, teachings or revelations to a position above the Bible. In doing so, they often deny or contradict the very thing they claim to uphold, the main historical source of all Jesus' teachings, the New Testament. (Why claim to be "Christian," or sympathetic to Christianity, unless one is willing to give credence to what Jesus really taught?)

Some say the Bible has gotten watered down through the centuries making the need for new revelations necessary, but that is not a tenable position either. There are over 24,600 partial or complete manuscripts of the New Testament. (The second-best documented manuscript of ancient history is the *Iliad and the Odyssey,* by Homer. It has only 643 manuscripts.) Even if all of the New Testament manuscripts were destroyed, we could still reconstruct all of the New Testament, with the exception of about eleven verses, from the writings of the early church fathers, all done before the year A.D. 325. Even non-Christian historians have to admit that by all scientific and historical standards applied to any ancient document, the New Testament is *over* ninety-nine percent accurate. Anyone can dispute its message, not so its historicity.[1]

The Bible claims to be the final authority for determining matters of doctrine (2 Timothy 3:16,17). For Christians, any book or writing or teaching that would change the content of the Bible is to be rejected. Scripture is emphatic on this point. Jude wrote, ". . . I felt the necessity to write to you appealing that you contend earnestly for the faith which was *once for all* delivered to the saints" (Jude 3).[2] Scripture makes no allowance for further teachings that would alter or add to the Bible. Paul said, ". . . even though we, or an angel from heaven, should preach to you a gospel contrary to that which we have preached to you, let him be accursed" (Galatians 1:8, compare Revelation 22:19; Deuteronomy 4:2).

If other sources are to make claims of divine inspiration, as the Bible does, then they must be measured in light of the Bible. God cannot contradict Himself. Thus, whatever these later speakers or writers claim must not contradict the Bible, which we already know to be true. If they do, it becomes clear that they are not speaking by God's inspiration either verbally or in written form.

In considering the deity of Christ, the issue is not whether the deity of Christ is easy to believe or even to understand, but whether it is taught in God's Word. If at first the idea appears incompatible with human reason or understanding, that does not automatically rule out the possibility of its being true. Our universe is full of things (like gravity, the nature of light, quasars) that are beyond human understanding at this time, but nonetheless true. The Bible teaches that God is incomprehensible to human minds (Job 11:7; 42:2-6; Psalm 145:3; Isaiah 40:13; 55:8, 9; Romans 11:33). Therefore, God must be allowed to have the final word on Himself, whether we can fully understand it or not.

Concerning God's revelation of Himself in the person of Jesus, Scripture says,

> God, after He spoke long ago to the fathers in the prophets in many portions and in many ways, in these last days has spoken to us in His Son, whom He appointed heir of all things, through whom also He made the world. And He is the radiance of His glory and the exact representation of His nature, and upholds all things by the word of His power (Hebrews 1:1-3).

Jesus Christ is the *living* Word of God. He reveals the Father. When one of his followers said, "Show us the Father" (John 14:8), Jesus answered, "Have I been so long with you, and yet you have not come to know me . . . ? He who has seen Me has seen the Father" (v.9). The apostle Paul called Jesus the "image of the invisible God" (Colossians 1:15). Thus, as will be discussed in this book, to look at Jesus and listen to Him is the same as looking at and listening to God.

What Are the Issues?

If Christ was God in the form of a man, then He, as no other human being in history, is to be listened to, revered, and even worshiped. It would mean that the God who created the galaxies, nebuli, and quasars, who cast billions of suns into the heavens, that God became a man, lived and walked on this earth, and died in submission to His own creation. His death would mean infinitely more than the death of a good man. It would be the supreme sacrifice of all time, a manifestation of unfathomable love. To treat

Jesus as a mere man (or even a god) under such circumstances would be blasphemy. To fail to adjust one's life
to His teaching would be to miss life itself.

On the other hand, if Jesus were *not* God but a lower
created being, one might feel gratitude for His life,
death, and teachings. But to worship Him as God would
be a tremendous mistake; He would be no more than
an idol occupying the place of God. The Bible is clear
about idolatry. God says that He will not give His glory
to another (Isaiah 42:8; 48:11), that there are no other
gods (or Gods) beside Himself (Isaiah 45:5, 21, 22;
Jeremiah 10:6, 1 Corinthians 8:4-6), and that we are to
worship God alone (Deuteronomy 6:13, 14; Matthew
4:10). So, either Jesus is God or He is not. To believe
in Him wrongly is a form of either blasphemy or idolatry.

This discussion can get complicated, depending on
what a person has been taught. Arguments can be made
both for and against the deity of Christ. For example,
if one has been taught that God is one person and that
Jesus is a created being, then on first reading, Bible
verses can be found to support that view. On the other
hand, if one has been taught that God is one supreme
being comprised of Father, Son, and Holy Spirit, and
that the Son gave up His position of equality within the
godhead to become a man in the person of Jesus, then
Scripture passages can be found to support that view.
So, the question is not whether either position has an
apparent case to make, but rather, which has the *best*
evidence? Which one does Scripture actually teach?

In considering the two sides, we believe that we are
able to give more than adequate responses to all verses
used to argue that Jesus is not God. We will show that
Scripture ascribes to Jesus *every* major name, attribute,
and title of God: We will show from Scripture that Jesus
received worship and prayer and we will give answers

to all major counter-arguments. We will document from church history (prior to the Nicene Council in A.D. 325 at which time this became the official position of the church) that belief in Jesus' divinity has *always* been the orthodox view.

Obviously both views cannot be right. It would be much easier if it were only a matter of sincerity, but it is not. It is a matter of which is *true* (Romans 10:2).

Definition of Terms

Adequate definitions of the nature of God, the nature of the Trinity, and the person and nature of Jesus Christ are prerequisite to understanding the many Scriptures concerning the deity of Christ.

1. God: The Scriptures teach that God is personal, intelligent, loving, just, faithful, eternal, creative, and in dynamic interaction with His creation. The attributes of God can be summarized into two groups: *general* attributes and *moral* attributes. Robert Passantino states, "God [according to His general attributes] is unique, eternal, immutable, omnipotent, omniscient, omnipresent, triune, spirit, and personal."[3] He continues, "The moral attributes of God include his holiness, righteousness, love and truth."[4] Christianity teaches that God sustains and sovereignly rules the universe in the present, and, as we will try to show, became incarnate in Jesus of Nazareth.

2. Trinity: Out of all reality or existence, only God is tripersonal or triune. When we say that God is triune, we are labeling the view of God derived from a panorama of Scripture passages that describe the personal nature of God. By triune, from which the word Trinity comes, we mean that God is consistently revealed as subsisting eternally as three persons (Father, Son, and Holy Spirit). These three persons make up the Godhead, yet there is only *one* God.

We do *not* mean:

(1) There is one God and three gods.
(2) There is one God and one person with three names or modes or manifestations.
(3) There is one God and one person who became three separate and successive persons.
(4) There are three gods who are in one "family."
(5) The one God is schizophrenic.

The biblical doctrine of the Trinity can be summarized as follows.

The one true God, as already established (Isaiah 43:10; Deuteronomy 6:4), is made up of Father, Son, and Holy Spirit. Each member of the godhead is called "God" in the Bible. The Father bears the name God (Galatians 1:1; Titus 1:4; etc.). The Son, or Word *(logos)*, is repeatedly called God in verses like John 1:1, 14; Acts 20:28; John 20:28; Titus 2:13; Hebrews 1:8, etc. The Holy Spirit is identified as God in various Scriptures (Acts 5:3-4; 1 John 4:2, 3; Hebrews 10:15, 16). The concept of the unity within the Trinity is seen in a verse such as Matthew 28:19, where the Father, Son, and Holy Spirit comprise one "name" (singular in Greek).

For the purposes of this book we are not attempting to defend the doctrine of the Trinity. Once a person comes to believe in the divinity of Christ, belief in God's existence as Father, Son, and Holy Spirit is usually not a problem. For the person wanting to research what the Bible says on the Trinity, many verses can be studied (Matthew 3:16, 17; Mark 1:9-11; Luke 1:35; 3:21, 22; John 3:34-36; 14:26; 16:13-15; Acts 2:32, 33; 38, 39; Romans 15:16, 30; 1 Corinthians 12:4-6; 2 Corinthians 3:4-6; 13:14; Ephesians 1:3-14; 2:18-22; 3:14-17; 4:4-6; 2 Thessalonians 2:13, 14;

1 Timothy 3:15, 16; Hebrews 9:14; 10:7; 10-15; 1 Peter 1:2; to name a few).

3. Jesus Christ: "Jesus Christ" is both a name and a title. The name *Jesus* is derived from the Greek form of the name *Jeshua* or *Joshua* meaning "Jehovah-Savior" or "the Lord saves." The title *Christ* is derived from the Greek word for Messiah (or the Hebrew *Mashiach*—Daniel 9:26) and means "anointed one." Two offices, king and priest, are involved in the use of the title *Christ.* That title points to Jesus as the promised priest and king of Old Testament prophecies.

Beyond that, we believe that Jesus possesses two natures, the human and the divine; thus we hold the view that Jesus is fully God (in nature) and yet fully human— God revealed in human form.

The Bible describes Jesus' dual nature as both God and man like this:

> Have this attitude in yourselves which was also in Christ Jesus, who, although He existed in the *form of God* [His divine nature], did not regard *equality* with God [the Father] a thing to be grasped [held on to], but emptied Himself, taking the *form of a bond-servant* [form number two, his human nature], and being made in the likeness of men. And being found in appearance as a man, He humbled Himself by becoming obedient to the point of death, even death on a cross. Therefore also God [the Father] highly exalted Him, and bestowed on Him the name which is above every name, that at the name of Jesus every knee should bow [worship], of those who are in heaven, and on earth, and under the earth, and that every tongue should confess that Jesus Christ is Lord [God the Son], to the glory of God the Father (Philippians 2:5-11).

With these working definitions of God, the Trinity, and Jesus, we will try to answer one more question before we begin looking at the scriptural evidence for the deity of Christ.

Why Would God Become a Man?

How can finite human beings such as ourselves understand an infinite God? It would be hard for any of us to comprehend abstractions like truth, goodness, or beauty apart from visible examples of them. We come to know beauty as it is seen in a beautiful object, goodness as it is focused in a good person, and so forth. But what about God? How could anyone grasp what God is like?

We could to some extent if somehow God focused Himself in a form that human beings could understand—by being another human. Although that man in his lifetime would not express the eternalness and omnipresence of God (there would be neither time nor space for that), that man could visibly express the nature of God.

That is the message of the New Testament. Paul said that in Christ "*all* the fulness of *Deity* dwells *in bodily form*" (Colossians 2:9). Jesus became human so that human beings could have some understanding of the infinite God.

A second reason God chose to become a man was to bridge the gulf between God and humankind. If Jesus had been "only" a man or a created being, then the hugeness of the gulf between God and humanity—the infinite and the finite, the Creator and the created, the Holy and the unholy—would have remained. For us to be able to know God, God had to step down to us. No created being could have bridged the gigantic gap between God and human beings, any more than a piece of clay could aspire to understand and reach the level of the sculptor. Out of love, God took that step down to us. He wanted to open a way that all might come to know Him.

Chapter 2

Jesus Christ Possesses the Names and Titles of God

The strongest argument for the deity of Christ is the one that most incensed Jesus' contemporaries. He took to Himself the Old Testament names and titles for God and also allowed others to call Him by the same names and titles. When Jesus called Himself by those appellations of deity, it so angered the rulers of the Jews that they tried to kill Him for blasphemy. The Jewish authorities had no doubt. This Galilean teacher was claiming to be Almighty God.

One could object, saying that Jesus' claiming those divine names and titles did not make Him and God one and the same. Several people may have the same name and title. Or, John Smith can be a man, husband, friend, and vice president of sales, all at the same time. Some names and titles, however, are exclusive and can be held by only one person. For example, there can be only one President of the United States at any one time. Many of the names and titles that the Bible uses for Jesus were those that only one person could rightfully have—and that was God.

Yahweh (Jehovah)

Jesus claimed for Himself the name of God most revered by the Jews, a name considered so sacred that the Jews would not even utter it: YHWH (now often pronounced Yahweh or Jehovah).

God first revealed the meaning of this name to His people in Exodus 3. After Moses had asked God by what name God should be called, the Lord replied, "I AM WHO I AM. . . Thus you shall say to the sons of Israel, 'I AM has sent me to you'" (Exodus 3:13, 14).

The phrase I AM is *not* the word YHWH. However it is a derivative of the verb "to be," from which the divine name Yahweh (YHWH) is also derived in Exodus 3:15. Thus the I AM WHO I AM title which God gave to Moses is a fuller expression of His eternal being, shortened in v. 15 to the divine name of YHWH. The Septuagint, the Greek translation of the Hebrew Old Testament, translated the first use of the phrase I AM in Exodus 3:14 as *ego eimi.* (Greek was the spoken language of Jesus' day and is the language in which the New Testament was written.)

So, in the time of Jesus, the emphatic form of "I am" *(ego eimi)* in Greek was the equivalent of the Hebrew Yahweh. Depending on the context, it could be a forceful way of saying "I am!" (as in John 9:9), or it could be the name of God Himself, the eternal I AM.

On several occasions Jesus used the term *ego eimi* of Himself as it can be used only of God. The clearest example is when the Jews said to Jesus: "'You are not yet fifty years old, and have You seen Abraham?' Jesus said to them, 'Truly, truly, I say to you, before Abraham was born, I AM' [Greek: *ego eimi*]. Therefore they picked up stones to throw at Him" (John 8:57-59). The Jews sought to kill Him for the presumption of that claim to deity. The Old Testament was clear. The prescribed penalty for blasphemy was to be stoned to death (Leviticus 24:16).

Jesus ascribed this title to Himself in other instances as well. Earlier in the same chapter, Jesus declared: ". . . unless you believe that I am [*ego eimi*] He, you shall die in your sins" (John 8:24). In Greek the word *He* does not appear. It simply reads ". . . unless you believe that I am. . ." He told the Jews, "When you lift up the Son of Man, then you will know that I am [*ego eimi*] He" (John 8:28). Again the *He* is omitted in the Greek.

Jesus continually affirmed His deity. When Jewish temple guards, along with Roman soldiers, came to arrest Him the night before His crucifixion, Jesus asked them, "'Whom do you seek?' They answered Him, 'Jesus the Nazarene.' He said to them, 'I am [*ego eimi*] He.'. . . When therefore He said to them, 'I am He,' they drew back, and fell to the ground" (John 18:4-6). They were unable to stand before the force of His claim and the force of His person.

The New Testament writers, convinced that Jesus Christ was God, saw no conflict in ascribing to Jesus Old Testament passages that referred to YHWH (Jehovah).

Beginning his Gospel, Mark quoted Isaiah's reference to God: "A voice is calling, 'Clear the way for the LORD [Yahweh] in the wilderness; Make smooth in the desert a highway for our God'" (Isaiah 40:3). Mark interpreted that passage as having its fulfillment in John the Baptist's preparing the way for Jesus (Mark 1:2-4; compare John 1:23).

Paul quoted Joel 2:32, "And it will come about that whoever calls on the name of the LORD [Yahweh] will be delivered [saved]." Paul applied that quote to Jesus, writing about Him and saying, "for 'Whoever will call upon the name of the LORD will be saved'" (Romans 10:13).

Peter quoted the same verse from Joel. "Every one who calls on the name of the LORD shall be saved" (Acts 2:21). Then when the people asked what they had to do to be saved, Peter told them, "Repent, and let each of you be baptized in the name of Jesus Christ. . ." (Acts 2:38). Having just stated that calling upon the name of the Lord (Yahweh) was a prerequisite for salvation, Peter tells them to be baptized in the name of Jesus Christ. Had Peter not considered

Christ God, one would have expected him to tell them to be baptized in the name of Yahweh, which would have been consistent with Jewish practice and belief.

Perhaps more important than the fact that the disciples gave this designation to Jesus is that His enemies recognized that He was claiming to be God. A hostile witness is always strong evidence in a court of law. For example, as will be elaborated on later, Jesus said,

> "I and the Father are one." The Jews took up stones again to stone Him. Jesus answered them, "I showed you many good works from the Father; for which of them are you stoning me?" The Jews answered him, "For a good work we do not stone You, but for blasphemy; and because You, being a man, make Yourself out to be God" (John 10:30-33).

There was no doubt as to who the Jewish leaders thought Jesus was making Himself out to be. Thus, the main accusation of Jesus' enemies centered not on what He did, but rather on who He claimed to be: God.

God

The Greek word used hundreds of times in the New Testament for *God* is the word *Theos* (corresponding to the Hebrew *Elohim* in the Old Testament). Jesus is called by that name in distinction to false gods in a number of instances.

The biblical Judeo-Christian view of one true God stands in contrast to Hindu and Buddhist religions which, respectively, identify man's true self as one with God or with ultimate reality. For example, most Hindu gurus in this country have no problem in saying, "I am God," and in teaching their thousands of followers likewise. Obviously one who believes he is inwardly already God has no need to seek God in the Christian sense, or to accept a personal Savior. Such is not the case with the New Testament, set in the Jewish, monotheistic framework which clearly delineates between God and His creation. Culturally, Jesus could not have been called by the name God unless he was considered to be the "one God" (Deuteronomy 6:4), since in Jewish thinking there were no "other gods."

C.S. Lewis writes:

> One attempt consists in saying that the Man did not really say these things, but that His followers exaggerated the story, and so the legend grew up that He had said them. This is difficult because His followers were all Jews; that is, they belonged to that nation which of all others was most convinced that there was only one God—that there could not possibly be another. It is very odd that this horrible invention about a religious leader should grow up among the one people in the whole earth least likely to make such a mistake. On the contrary we get the impression that none of His immediate followers or even of the New Testament writers embraced the doctrine at all easily.[1]

God stood separate from His creation. Human beings were not an extension of God.

Following are eleven New Testament examples where Christ is called God.

1. In Hebrews 1, in which Christ's supremacy over angels and prophets is presented, the writer of Hebrews said, "But of the *Son* He [God] says, 'Thy throne, *O God* [*Theos*], is forever and ever.'" Hebrews 1:8, just quoted, is a direct quote from Psalm 45:6, 7 where "God" is addressing "God."

As translated, Hebrews 1:8 is a correct rendering of the Greek text despite how it is translated in some versions.[2]

2. Peter called Christ "God" (*Theos*). He wrote, "Simon Peter, a bond-servant and apostle of Jesus Christ . . . by the righteousness *of our God and Savior,* Jesus Christ" (2 Peter 1:1), the phrase Jesus Christ here acting as an appositive to God and Savior. (An appositive in Greek means that a noun or a noun phrase is used with another as an explanatory equivalent).

In the original New Testament Greek, this is called a Granville Sharpe construction. One article covers both nouns (*God* and *Savior*). The Greek conjunction "*and*" (Greek: *kai*) couples the two nouns inseparably. This means that the appositive (the word that renames), Jesus Christ, *must* refer to both *God* and *Savior.* Jesus Christ *is* our God and Savior. Grammarians are emphatic that only one person is meant, not two. Winer Schmeidel's *Grammatik* (p. 158) says, "Grammar demands that one person be meant"; A. T. Robertson's *Word Pictures in the New Testament* (Vol. 6, p. 147) states, "One person not two." (Compare Moulton's *Grammar,* Vol. 3, p. 181, and Dana and Mantey's *A Manual Grammar of NT Greek,* p. 147.) All agree that Jesus Christ is the "great God and Savior."

3. The same Granville Sharpe construction was also used by Paul as he told Titus to await the "appearing of the glory of our great God and Savior, Christ Jesus" (Titus 2:13).

4. Thomas, who doubted the resurrection, said, "Unless I shall see in His hands the imprint of the nails, and put my finger into the place of the nails, and put my hand into His side, I will not believe" (John 20:25). When Jesus appeared to Thomas, He said, "Reach here your finger, and see My hands; and reach here your hand, and put it into My side; and be not unbelieving, but believing" (v.27). Thomas replied, "My Lord and *My God* [*Theos*]!" (v.28).

There is no mistaking that Thomas's words were addressed to Jesus. Thomas used both titles to express his understanding of Christ's deity and lordship. Jesus did not rebuke Thomas for blasphemy. Instead, He accepted those titles of deity.

5. Acts 2:36 says, "God has made him [Jesus] both Lord and Christ." Verse 39 speaks of God as "the Lord our God," and thus Christ who is Lord (v.36) is also God (v.39). Acts 10:36 reinforces this point, referring to Christ as "Lord of all."

6. Acts 16:31 and 34 refer to belief in the Lord Jesus as belief in God.

7. Revelation 7:10-12, 17 reads: "And they cry out with a loud voice, saying, 'Salvation to our God who sits on the throne, and to the Lamb.' And all the angels were standing around the throne and around the elders and the four living creatures; and they fell on their faces before the throne and worshiped God, saying, 'Amen, blessing and glory and wisdom and thanksgiving and honor and power and might, be to our God forever and ever. Amen.'. . . for the Lamb in the center of the throne shall be their shepherd, and shall guide them to springs of the water of life; and God shall wipe every tear from their eyes." Note that in verse 10 it is God who sits on the throne and in verse 17 it is the Lamb (Jesus) in the center of the throne. Who is in the center of the throne? To say that Jesus is at the center and yet deny His divinity is to rob God of the central place in heaven, an untenable position.

8. In Acts 18, the "way of the Lord . . . the things concerning Jesus" (v.25) is the same as the "way of God" (v.26).

9. Another name for the Messiah was the name *Immanuel* (Isaiah 7:14), which translated literally means "God with us." In Matthew 1:23 this title is clearly assigned to

Jesus: "Behold, the virgin shall be with child, and shall bear a Son, and they shall call His name Immanuel, which translated means, 'God with us.'"

10. Isaiah 9:6 reads, "For a child will be born to us, a son will be given to us; and the government will rest on His shoulders; and His name will be called Wonderful Counselor, Mighty God, Eternal Father, Prince of Peace." This prophecy concerning Jesus, the Messiah, indicates that one of His names will be "Mighty *God,*" which is the Hebrew *El Gibbor.* The same phrase is used of Yahweh in Isaiah 10:21. The point is that the Holy Spirit designated the child Jesus with such names. If the names were not intended to express the child's nature, it would be deception. "His name will be called" means "This is what He is," not "this is what His name means, but He is not that which it states."

As Herbert C. Leupold says, "This is the type of character that will be his . . . he is called by these names because he actually *is* the kind of person the names say he is."[3] If Jesus is not mighty God, neither is He "Wonderful Counselor" or the "Prince of Peace." And if He is not one of these, why use such terms at all? Why tell us the meaning of a name if it has no relevance? But, as the rest of Isaiah and the Old Testament point out, the Messiah *is* a wonderful counselor and a prince of peace (Isaiah 42 and 49; compare Zechariah 9:9, 10; Micah 5:4). And as the New Testament proves, He is also Almighty God (John 1:1; Titus 2:13).

11. John 1:1, 14 reads, "In the beginning was the Word, and the Word was with God, and the Word was God [*Theos*] . . . And the Word became flesh, and dwelt among us." There is not a more widely used nor more highly controversial passage about Christ's deity than John 1:1. There is little question that the "Word" refers to Jesus, since verse 14 says, "And the Word became flesh, and dwelt among us." Taken at face value, verses 1 and 14 teach the deity

of Christ; they state that the Word was "with God," "was God," and "became flesh."

To deny the deity of Christ after reading those verses, one would have to mistranslate or reinterpret John 1:1. One way John 1:1 is mistranslated is by rendering the phrase "the Word was God" as "the Word was *a* god. The problem with this translation is that the Greek text does not warrant the use of the indefinite article "a" before "God."

Bruce Metzger, a student of the Greek language, relates a study of the Greek definite article done by Dr. Ernest Cadman Colwell of the University of Chicago. Colwell writes that

> "A definite predicate nominative has the article when it follows the verb; it does not have the article when it precedes the verb . . . The opening verse of John's Gospel contains one of the many passages where this rule suggests the translation of a predicate as a definite noun. The absence of the article (before *theos*) does *not* make the predicate indefinite or qualitative when it precedes the verb; it is indefinite in this position only when the context demands it. The context makes no such demand in the Gospel of John, for this statement cannot be regarded as strange in the prologue of the gospel which reaches its climax in the confession of Thomas."[4]

F. F. Bruce, an expert in biblical languages, says that rendering the phrase as "a god" is a frightful mistranslation because the omission of the indefinite article is common with nouns in the predicative construction.[5]

Thus, John 1:1 is one of the clearest verses in the New Testament expressing the absolute deity of Christ. The construction has been discussed by many of the world's great Greek and biblical scholars. We might paraphrase the verse something like this: "Before anything came into existence, the Word was already in existence. He enjoyed a close relationship to God, and what God was, the Word was."

As F. F. Bruce says of verse 1, ". . . The force is 'and the Word was Himself God.'"[6]

Sometimes people ask how Jesus could be "God" and "with God" at the same time. The response to that is found in the concept of the Trinity: one God in three eternal persons. The *Word* of John 1:1 was with the other persons of the Trinity and is Himself God by nature.

A group known as The Way International interprets Jesus' being the "Word" in the sense that He was an expression of God in the way that our words are an expression of ourselves. The Way does not believe that Jesus was the Word in the sense of being God. To support this interpretation, adherents say that John 1:1-18 is primarily speaking of God, not Jesus; that if these verses were speaking of Jesus, they would be attributing to Jesus characteristics that only God could have. Thus, as much as possible, they try to take Jesus out of the limelight, saying that the overall thrust of John 1 is to point to God.

There are problems with their interpretation, though. First, the string of pronouns *He* and *Him* in John 1 make little sense if they refer mainly to God rather than Jesus, since the whole thrust of John's Gospel is that people might believe in *Jesus.* In the Gospel's key verse, John said, ". . . these have been written that you may believe that Jesus is the Christ, the Son of God" (John 20:31). It seems logical, therefore, that John's introduction would tie in with his main theme.

Second, all that is spoken of in the first 18 verses of John 1 is repeated about Jesus elsewhere in the Gospel or in other New Testament passages. Some examples:

Chapter One	*Parallel Passages*
Verses 3 and 10: *He* created the world	Jesus was active in creating the world (Hebrews 1:1, 2, 8-13; Colossians 1:16-18).

Verse 4: "in *Him* was life"

Jesus said He was the "bread of *life*," "the resurrection and the *life*," "the way, and the truth, and the *life*" (John 6:35, 48, 51; 11:25; 14:6). John 20:31 states that people can have *life* by believing in Jesus.

Verses 4 and 9: *He* was the "light of men" and the "true light"

Jesus said He is the "*light* of the world" (John 8:12; 9:5).

Verse 10: "*He* was in the world"

Who? Logically, the verse points to Jesus. Throughout the rest of John's Gospel, the emphasis is on Jesus coming into the world (John 3:17; 6:33, etc.).

Verse 11: "*He* came to *His* own, and those who were *His* own did not receive *Him*."

The Jews rejected Jesus, not God as they understood God (see John 3:32). In rejecting Jesus they thought they were doing God's will.

Verse 12: "But as many as received *Him*, to them He gave the right to become children of God, even to those who believe in *His* name.

Throughout this Gospel, John makes clear that people are to believe in Jesus (John 3:16-18; 5:24; 12:44; 20:31, etc.). Jesus bestows eternal life (John 10:28).

Alpha and Omega:
the First and the Last

The terms *Alpha* and *Omega* give a beautiful, awesome description of God. Long before the stars filled the heavens and our universe existed, God was. He is from everlasting to everlasting. Genesis 1:1 says, "In the beginning God. . ." God alone deserves the titles *Alpha* (the first) and *Omega* (the last).

Thus, these names express the eternal nature of God. He is the source and goal of all creation. No created being could ever rightfully claim to be the first and last of all that is.

Jesus and God are both called the Alpha and Omega, the first and the last, in Scripture.

God	*Jesus*
Isaiah 41:4—"I, the Lord [Yahweh], am the first, and with the last, I am He."	Revelation 1:17, 18— ". . . I am the first (*protos*) and the last (*eschatos*), and the living One; and I was dead, and behold, I am alive forevermore. . . ."
Isaiah 48:12—"I am He, I am the first, I am also the last."	Revelation 2:8—"And to the angel of the church in Smyrna write: "The first and the last, who was dead, and has come to life."
Revelation 1:8—""I am the Alpha and the Omega,' says the Lord God, 'who is and who was and who is to come, the Almighty.'"	Revelation 22:12-16— "Behold, I am coming quickly. . . I am the Alpha and the Omega, the first and the last, the beginning and the end . . . I, Jesus, have sent My angel to testify to you these things. . . ."
Revelation 21:6, 7—"I am the Alpha and the Omega, the beginning and the end. I will give to the one who thirsts from the spring of the water of life without cost. He who overcomes shall inherit these things, and I will be his God and he will be My son."	

The significance of the above passages in the book of Revelation cannot be underestimated. They are some of the strongest and clearest examples of Christ's claim to deity. There cannot be two first and two lasts, two Alphas and Omegas.

Lord

The title *Lord* is freely used in both Testaments to refer to God and Jesus. In the Old Testament the Hebrew word for Lord was *Adonai*. In the Septuagint and the New Testament the word translated "Lord" is *Kurios*. Both *Adonai* and *Kurios* were used for God by the Jews.

In the New Testament *Kurios* had two meanings, one common and one sacred. The common usage was a courteous greeting meaning "sir" or "master." The sacred sense implied deity. Some New Testament passages obviously use the word *Lord* as a term of respect for Jesus (John 4:11). Because the early Christians were monotheistic, as were the Jews, if they used the word *Lord* in the sacred sense for Jesus, it would be strong evidence that they thought Christ was God. As Hogg and Vine state,

> The full significance of this association of Jesus with God under the one appellation, 'Lord,' is seen when it is remembered that these men belonged to the only monotheistic race in the world. To associate with the Creator one known to be a creature, however exalted, though possible to Pagan philosophers, was quite impossible to a Jew.[7]

Romans who worshiped the emperor as a god would

often greet one another and say "Caesar is Lord." One reason the early Christians and Jews were persecuted was that they refused to give that honor to the emperor. That practice may also explain the significance of the Christian phrase, "Jesus is Lord" i.e., *Lord* being used in the sense of God.

There are several clear examples where Jesus is called "Lord" in the sacred sense in Scripture. Paul wrote, "No one speaking by the Spirit of God . . . can say, 'Jesus is Lord,' except by the Holy Spirit" (1 Corinthians 12:3). Some individuals might object by saying "I believe in Jesus as 'my Lord' but I certainly do not think he is God." The important question is what is meant by the word *Lord.* Anyone can mouth the words "Jesus is Lord" and some even mean it in the sense of master, but that is not what Paul was talking about. Several things indicate that Paul was making a statement about Jesus' divinity.

1. Paul began chapter 12 of 1 Corinthians by speaking of spiritual gifts and the fact that the Corinthians had been led into the worship of idols *as gods.* In contrast to those false gods (vv. 1, 2), Paul stated that no one by the Spirit of God can say "Jesus is accursed" and no one can affirm "Jesus is Lord" except by the Holy Spirit, implying that Jesus, the Lord, is the *true God* worthy of worship.

2. In verse 3, Paul treated the Spirit, Jesus and God on an equal basis. Verses 4-6 also show:

verse 4: varieties of gifts, but the same *Spirit*;

verse 5: varieties of ministries, and the same *Lord* (i.e., Jesus, verse 1);

verse 6: varieties of effects, but the same *God.* If Jesus is not God, why is he treated equally in verse 5? In verses 11 and 18 the Spirit and God are again treated as synonymous.

If one were to ask a person who denies the deity of Christ if he or she "prays to the *Lord*" that person would have to ask, "Whom do you mean?" That is the point. Throughout the New Testament, God and Jesus are both called Lord. The general answer he or she would be apt to give is "I pray to God, but I don't believe in praying to Jesus." In response, there are five New Testament examples where prayer is offered to Jesus in heaven as Lord (or the Son of God).

1. In Acts 7:59, 60 Stephen called on Jesus as Lord. As he was being stoned, he prayed, "Lord Jesus, receive my spirit." That indicated his belief that Jesus was more than a man, powerful enough to receive his spirit. "Falling on his knees he cried out with a loud voice, 'Lord, do not hold this sin against them!'" A pious Hellenistic Jew would not pray to anyone less than God.

2. In 1 Corinthians 1:2 Paul wrote to the "saints. . . who in every place call upon the name of our Lord Jesus Christ, their Lord and ours."

3. In 2 Corinthians 12:8-9 as Paul spoke of his "thorn in the flesh," he said, "Concerning this I entreated the *Lord* three times that it might depart from me. And He has said to me, '*My grace* is sufficient for you, for power is perfected in weakness.' Most gladly, therefore, I will rather boast about my weaknesses, that the power of *Christ* may dwell in me."

4. In 1 John 5:13-15 we read: "These things I have written to you who believe in the name of the *Son of God,* in order that you may know that you have eternal life. And this is the confidence which we have before Him, that, if we ask anything according to His will, *He hears us.* And if we know that He hears us in whatever we ask, we know that we have the request which we have *asked from Him.*" The pronouns *He* and *Him* refer to the Son of God (v.13).

5. In Acts 8:24 Simon said, "Pray to the *Lord*. . ." (in Verse 16 Jesus is the "Lord.")

Peter and Paul each made the assertion that Jesus is "Lord of all" (Acts 10:36; Romans 10:12). Paul also said, ". . . for if they had understood it, they would not have crucified the Lord of glory" (1 Corinthians 2:8). Who is the Lord of glory? Psalm 24:10 states that "The LORD [YHWH] of hosts, He is the King of glory." (See also Psalm 96:7, 8.)

In 2 Corinthians 4:4-5, Paul called Jesus Lord, saying, "The god of this world [Satan] has blinded the minds of the unbelieving, that they might not see the light of the gospel of the glory of Christ, who is the image of God. For we do not preach ourselves but Christ Jesus as Lord." Thus, Christ, the image of God, is *Lord.*

Paul used the same language and imagery in calling Jesus Lord that Isaiah used in the Old Testament of Yahweh (Jehovah):

God	*Jesus*
"I am *God* and there is no other. . . to Me *every knee will bow, every tongue will swear allegiance.* They will say of Me, 'Only in the Lord are righteousness and strength'" (Isaiah 45:22-24).	". . . at the name of *Jesus every knee should bow. . .* and that *every tongue should confess* that *Jesus Christ is Lord"* (Philippians 2:10-11).

Paul, an Old Testament scholar and Pharisee, would not have used that parallel by accident.

Jesus referred to Himself as "Lord of the Sabbath," a reference to Himself as the creator of the sabbath. In Exodus 31:13, 17 God said, "You shall surely observe My sabbaths; for this is a sign between Me and you. . . It is a sign between

Me and the sons of Israel forever." For the Jew, Yahweh was both author and Lord of the sabbath. When some Pharisees rebuked Jesus for allowing His disciples to pick grain on the sabbath, thus breaking the law, by "working," He said that it was all right because he was "Lord of the Sabbath" (Matthew 12:8). As C. S. Lewis says,

> Here is another curious remark: In almost every religion there are unpleasant observances like fasting. This Man suddenly remarks one day, "No one need fast while I am here." Who is this Man who remarks that His mere presence suspends all normal rules? Who is the person who can suddenly tell the school they can have a half holiday?[8]

The Jews who heard Him considered His words blasphemy. Then, that same sabbath day, He went into their synagogue and made a point again of "working," healing a man, which further infuriated them. That, too, was breaking the sabbath according to their understanding. Incensed at His claiming authority that only God could have, they tried to kill Him (Matthew 12:14).

To reiterate, according to Deuteronomy 6:4 and Mark 12:29, there can be only one Lord.

Savior

The God of the Old Testament stated unequivocally that He alone is the *Savior*. "I, even I, am the LORD [Yahweh]; And there is no savior besides me" (Isaiah 43:11). Yet Scripture explicitly states that Jesus is also *savior*.

God	Jesus
Isaiah 43:3—"I am the LORD [Yahweh] your God . . . your Savior."	Matthew 1:21 ". . . you shall call His name Jesus, for it is He who will save His people from their sins." John 1:29—"The next day he saw Jesus . . . and said, 'Behold, the Lamb of God who takes away the sin of the world!'"
1 Timothy 4:10—". . . we have fixed our hope on the living God, who is the Savior of all . . ."	John 4:42—". . . this One is indeed the Savior of the world." Hebrews 5:9—". . . He became to all those who obey Him the source of eternal salvation."
Luke 1:47—"And my spirit has rejoiced in God my Savior."	Luke 2:11—"For today in the city of David there has been born for you a Savior, who is Christ the Lord."

Paul told Titus to await the blessed hope, the "appearing of the glory of our great *God and Savior, Christ Jesus*" (Titus 2:13). The context of that verse is important. Within a span of twelve verses, Paul uses the phrases "God our Savior" and "Jesus our Savior" interchangeably four times (Titus 2:10, 13; 3:4, 6).

King

King is a title that expresses the majesty of God. The Psalmist wrote, "For the LORD is a great God, and a great

King above all gods" (Psalm 95:3). God said, "I am the LORD, your Holy One, the Creator of Israel, your King" (Isaiah 43:15). More than thirty times in Psalms, Isaiah, Jeremiah, Daniel, Zechariah, and Malachi, God is spoken of as the "King," "King of Israel," and "Great King."

While it is true that the term *king* is often a human title, the New Testament not only speaks of Christ as King in the same sense that the Old Testament describes God, but Jesus is called "King of kings." ". . . the Lamb [Jesus] will overcome them, because he is Lord of lords and King of kings" (Revelation 17:14). At Christ's second coming, the words KING OF KINGS, AND LORD OF LORDS will be written on His robe (Revelation 19:16). In the Old Testament, Yahweh (Jehovah) is referred to as the "God of gods and LORD of lords" (Deuteronomy 10:17).

First Timothy 6:14-16 has special importance. It reads, ". . . until the appearing of our Lord Jesus Christ, which He will bring about at the proper time—He who is the blessed and *only Sovereign,* the *King of kings* and *Lord of lords;* who *alone* possesses immortality and dwells in unapproachable light; whom no man has seen or can see." The *He* modified by "King of kings and Lord of lords" can refer to either Christ or God. If this does speak of Christ in His glorified state (Revelation 1:12-18), then He would be "only Sovereign," "King of kings," "Lord of lords," the only one to possess "immortality," and the one who "dwells in unapproachable light"—all titles of deity. On the other hand, if this passage speaks of God, then both Christ and God share the identical titles "King of kings and Lord of lords," as other passages previously mentioned indicate (Revelation 17:14). Either way, it argues for Christ's divinity.

Judge

The Old Testament left no doubt that God is the *judge*

of each person's soul. "He summons the heavens above, and the earth, to judge His people. . . for God Himself is judge" (Psalm 50:4, 6). There are many references to Yahweh (Jehovah) as judge (e.g., Genesis 18:25; Psalm 96:13; Hebrews 12:23, 24; 1 Peter 1:17). Yet in the New Testament, God the Father has left "all judgment to the Son" (John 5:22). The *reason* all judgment is given to the Son is stated in the next verse: "in order that all may honor the Son *even* as they honor the Father." Is the Father honored as God? Of course. So the Son must be honored likewise.

This entire passage (John 5:17-30) is one of the strongest composite statements of Christ's deity in the entire Bible. Jesus is the one who will "judge the living and the dead" (2 Timothy 4:1). It is before the "judgment seat of Christ" that all believers will appear (2 Corinthians 5:10). Romans 14:10 uses "judgment seat of God" in identical fashion. Both Christ and Yahweh search the hearts of believers (Revelation 2:23; Jeremiah 17:10). Thus Jesus and Yahweh stand as one judge.

Light

Light is used often to refer metaphorically to God and His presence or revelation. God is the "light," "Everlasting Light," "the light of the nations," "the one who lights our paths" and "illumines the darkness" (Psalm 27:1; Isaiah 42:6; 60:19, 20; 2 Samuel 22:29).

Jesus made a strong statement that He was the light, not one who merely pointed the way to the light. He said, "I am [*Ego eimi*] the light of the world; he who follows Me shall not walk in the darkness, but shall have the light of life" (John 8:12). Referring to Himself, Jesus also said, "And this is the judgment, that *the* light is come into the world, and men loved the darkness rather than the light" (John 3:19). He said, "While I am in the world, I am the light of the world" (John 9:5). The apostle John spoke of Jesus as the "light of men," the "true light," and the one who "enlightens every man" (John 1:4, 9). Just as God is eternal light, so is Jesus (Isaiah 60:19, 20; Revelation 21:23; 22:5).

Rock

Rock can mean many things, but when it becomes a name for God it symbolizes God's comfort, solidity, and strength. Just prior to his death, Moses left the children of Israel with a song reminding them of who God was and what God had done for them. Two names for God he used were Yahweh and Rock. "I proclaim the name of the Lord [Yahweh]. Ascribe greatness to our God! The Rock!" (Deuteronomy 32:3-4; see also Deuteronomy 32:15, 18, 30-31). The Psalmist called God the rock of my (or our) salvation (Psalm 89:26; 95:1). David worshiped God as a "rock" and the "Rock of Israel" (2 Samuel 22:2, 3, 47; 23:3). In 2 Samuel 22:32 a rhetorical question is asked: "For who is God, besides the Lord? And who is a rock, besides our God?"

In the New Testament, Jesus is given the title "Rock." Paul referred to the children of Israel in the wilderness with Moses, writing, "All ate the same spiritual food; and all drank the same spiritual drink, for they were drinking from a spiritual rock which followed them; and the rock was Christ" (1 Corinthians 10:3, 4; see Exodus 17:6; Nehemiah 9:15). Paul was referring symbolically here to the children of Israel's being nourished by God—manna from

Yahweh (v.3), drink from Christ (v.4). Thus, in Paul's thinking, Jesus was Yahweh.

Paul also spoke of Jesus as a "rock of offense" (Romans 9:33). Peter referred to Him as a "living stone," "a rock of offense," "a choice stone, a precious corner stone," and the "stone which the builders rejected" (1 Peter 2:4-8).

Redeemer

The word *redeemer* means one who purchases or buys back. When humankind was spiritually bankrupt, unable to save itself, God the Father willingly and by predetermination (Acts 2:23) sacrificed His Son for the redemption of all, opening the door for anyone to be reconciled to God. Scripture says that God is a God of "abundant redemption" (Psalm 130: 7, 8), the "Redeemer" (Isaiah 48:17; 54:5; 63:9), and the one who "redeems" our lives from "the pit" (Psalm 103:4). Ultimate redemption from sin can come only from God.

Jesus Christ is our redeemer from sin. "We have redemption through His blood, the forgiveness of our trespasses" (Ephesians 1:7). Jesus is the one who has purchased our "eternal redemption" (Hebrews 9:12). Paul told the elders at Ephesus to "shepherd the church of God which He purchased [redeemed] *with His own blood*" (Acts 20:28). That could refer only to Christ's death on the cross. Jesus Christ is God the Son our Redeemer.

The Lord Our Righteousness

Because of humanity's need for righteousness and our inability to meet God's standard of righteousness (Romans 3:23), the Old Testament prophesied that one day Yahweh would raise up a "righteous branch" from the root of David who would have the name "The LORD [Yahweh] our righteousness" (Jeremiah 23:6; 33:15, 16). According to Old Testament teaching, that branch is the Messiah, or Christ (compare Luke 1:32). One of Jesus' names therefore is "Yahweh our righteousness." Isaiah 45:24 tells us that "only in the LORD [Yahweh] are righteousness and strength."

Husband

One of the beautiful aspects of the title *husband,* when it is used for God, is that it reminds us that God's love longs to fill the emptiness and loneliness of people's hearts the way a loving husband meets his wife's needs (and vice versa). Isaiah reminded Israel of this truth when he told them, "For your husband is your Maker" (Isaiah 54:5). In the book of Hosea, God's love for Israel is compared with a faithful husband's loving an unfaithful wife. God gave the promise that even though judgment was coming, Israel would once again call Him *husband* (Hosea 2:16).

Just as God is the "husband" of Israel, the New Testament sees Jesus as the "husband" of the church. Christ said His disciples were justified in not fasting since He was the "bridegroom" (Mark 2:18, 19). In Matthew 25:1 the virgins (the church) are told to await the "bridegroom," Jesus. In 2 Corinthians 11:2, Paul said the church is betrothed to "*one* husband, that to Christ." In Revelation 21:2, 9, Jesus is referred to as the "husband" of his "bride," the new Jerusalem, in heaven. Like God, Jesus Christ is the divine husband.

Shepherd

A beautiful term for God and His care for human beings is *shepherd.* "The Lord is my shepherd, I shall not want. . .," David sang (Psalm 23:1). Psalm 80:1 reads, "Oh give ear, Shepherd of Israel, Thou who dost lead Joseph like a flock." Genesis 49:24 refers to God as the "Shepherd, the Stone of Israel." Ezekiel devoted a whole chapter to God as "shepherd" to the lost house of Israel, the sheep of His pasture (Ezekiel 34).

Although the use of the term *shepherd* does not prove Christ's deity, Peter and the author of Hebrews went so far as to call Jesus the "Chief Shepherd," the "great Shepherd of the sheep," and the "Shepherd and Guardian" of our souls (1 Peter 5:4; Hebrews 13:20; 1 Peter 2:25). Jesus also called Himself "shepherd," asserting that He was the "good shepherd" (John 10:11), the *one* shepherd (John 10:16).

Creator

The first verse in the Bible reads, "In the beginning God created the heavens and the earth" (Genesis 1:1). God is plainly identified as *creator.* To have said anything different would have been blasphemy to the Jews. Time after time God is said to have created the world (Job 33:4; Psalm 95:5, 6; 102:25, 26; Ecclesiastes 12:1; Isaiah 40:28).

The New Testament affirms Christ's deity by speaking of Him as *creator:*

> *He* [Jesus] was in the beginning with God. All things came into being through *Him;* and apart from *Him* nothing came into being that has come into being. . . *He* was in the world, and the world was made *through Him,* and the world did not know *Him* (John 1:2, 3, 10).

The string of connected pronouns make clear that the person being spoken of is Jesus.

Paul expressed the same thought:

> For in *Him* [Jesus] *all things were created,* both in the heavens and on earth, visible and invisible, whether thrones or dominions or rulers or authorities—all things have been created *through Him* and *for Him.* And *He* is before all things, and in *Him* all things hold together. *He* is also the head of the body, the church; and *He* is the beginning, the first-born from the dead..." (Colossians 1:16-18).

The text indicates that Paul was writing about Jesus. The connected pronouns refer to only one person. They speak of one person through whom "all things were created," who is "head of the church," "in the beginning," and is the "first born from the dead." According to Ephesians 5:23, John 1:1, and 1 Corinthians 15:20, Jesus was all of these things.

The writer of Hebrews underscored the same point. "God... in these last days has spoken to us in His Son, whom He appointed heir of all things, *through whom also He made the world*" (Hebrews 1:1,2). In the same chapter, as the "Son" (v.8) is still being addressed, the writer went on to state, "Thou Lord [Jesus], in the beginning didst lay the foundation of the earth, and the heavens are the *works of Thy hands*" (Hebrews 1:10).

Lewis Sperry Chafer states:

> In itself, the act of creating is an incomparable undertaking. In His creation of material things, God called them into existence out of nothing. Such a declaration is far removed from the notion that nothing has produced something. It is obvious that out of nothing nothing of itself could arise. The biblical declaration is rather that out of infinite resources of God everything has come into existence. He is the Source of all that is. The self-determining will of God

has caused the material universe, as stated in Romans 11:36, "For of him, and through him, and to him, are all things: to whom be glory for ever." In this Scripture the creation of all things is predicated of God; but, in Colossians 1:16-17, it is asserted in the same general terms that all things were created by Christ and for Him, that He is before all things and by Him all things are created.[9]

Giver of Life

The crowning moment of creation was when God "formed man... and breathed into his nostrils the breath of life" (Genesis 2:7). In Deuteronomy 32:39, after saying, "... there is no god besides me," God said He is the one to "give life" (compare Psalm 36:9).

Jesus said, "For just as the Father raises the dead and gives them life, even so the Son also gives life..." (John 5:21). Just prior to raising Lazarus from the dead, Jesus said, "I am the resurrection and the life" (John 11:25). He went so far as to say that He was the giver of eternal life. "I give eternal life to them, and they shall never perish; and no one shall snatch them out of my hand... I and the Father are one" (John 10:28-30). Jesus said that the Scriptures (referring to the Old Testament) "bear witness of Me; and you are unwilling to come to Me, that you may have *life*" (John 5:39,40).

Forgiver of Sins

God is the one who forgives "iniquity, transgression and sin" (Exodus 34:7; see also Nehemiah 9:17; Psalm 86:5; 130:4; Isaiah 55:7; Jeremiah 31:34; Daniel 9:9; Jonah 4:2). Jesus, God the Son, can forgive sin. Colossians 2:13 and 3:13 speak of Jesus as the one who forgives transgression.

Jesus said to Paul that to "receive forgiveness of sins" one must have "faith in Me" (Acts 26:18).

Some people sought healing from Him for their friend, a paralyzed man (Mark 2:1-12). As Jesus was teaching in a house, they lowered the man through a hole in the roof in such a way that he would lie at Jesus' feet. Touched by their belief in Him, Jesus said to the paralytic, "My son, your sins are forgiven." "What arrogance! What presumption!" some individuals in the crowd were thinking. How could Jesus know the paralyzed man's sins, much less offer forgiveness, as if, like God, the sins had been committed against Himself? As if He had the power? Jesus' response was clear. He was not being arrogant. He was speaking truth. Here was the proof: "In order that you may know that the Son of Man has authority on earth to forgive sins, . . . rise, take up your pallet and go home." The man did, and they were all amazed and glorified God.

Of this passage, Mark 2:7 in particular, Greek grammarian, A. T. Robertson states:

> It was, they held, blasphemy for Jesus to assume this divine prerogative. Their logic was correct. The only flaw in it was the possibility that Jesus held a peculiar relation to God which justified his claim. So the two forces clash here as now on the deity of Christ Jesus. Knowing full well that he had exercised the prerogative of God in forgiving the man's sins he proceeds to justify his claim by healing the man.[10]

Robert Alan Cole, in his commentary on Mark, states that the passage can be looked at in a number of different ways, but they all merge into only one meaning. He paraphrases the passage (vv.10,11) as he explains:

> These are two ways of understanding this passage; both

lines of exegesis are fruitful, and, if pursued far enough, merge into one. The first interpretation is to paraphrase, 'You say that only God can forgive sins? But I will show you that here is a *man* who has the same power,' thus leading the thoughtful scribe to the equation of the man Christ Jesus with God."[11]

In his lecture on forgiveness, one of the present authors, Josh McDowell, emphasizes:

This concept of forgiveness bothered me for quite awhile because I didn't understand it. One day in a philosophy class, answering a question about the deity of Christ, I quoted the above verses from Mark 2. A graduate assistant challenged my conclusion that Christ's forgiveness demonstrated His deity. He said that he could forgive someone but that wouldn't demonstrate he was claiming to be God. As I thought about what the graduate assistant was saying, it struck me why the religious leaders reacted against Christ. Yes, one can say, "I forgive you," but that can be done only by the person who was sinned against. In other words, if you sin against me, I can say, "I forgive you." But that wasn't what Christ was doing. The paralytic had sinned against God the Father, and then Jesus, under His own authority, said, "Your sins are forgiven." Certainly we can forgive injuries committed against us, but in no way can anyone forgive sins committed against God except God Himself. That is what Jesus said.

Jesus' power to forgive sin is a startling example of His exercising a prerogative that belongs to God alone.

The Lord Our Healer

In Exodus 15:26 Yahweh said, "I, the LORD, am your

healer." Although it is true that God has given the gift of healing to men and women throughout the ages, never has anyone claimed to heal through personal authority, as Jesus did. The early disciples believed in that authority, and they healed and cast out demons in the name of Jesus (Matthew 10:1; Mark 9:38; Luke 10:17). Jesus' enemies were horrified (John 9:24). Who in his right mind would say he was healing and casting out demons in his own name? That would be taking glory that belonged only to God.

As part of His healing power, Jesus also claimed that He had authority over demonic powers (Matthew 12:22-29), a fact that the defeated demons conceded, acknowledging Him as the "Holy One of God" and the "Son of God" (Mark 1:24; 5:7; Luke 4:34). The early church agreed, teaching that all angels, authorities, and powers were in submission to Him (1 Peter 3:22). In Acts 9:34, when Peter encountered a paralyzed man he called the man by name and said, "Aeneas, Jesus Christ heals you." And He did. Here, Jesus in heaven, was acting as healer, as God.

Thus, Scripture speaks in a strong voice. Jesus claimed for Himself, and was called by others, names and titles that only God could rightfully bear: Yahweh, God, Alpha and Omega, Lord, Savior, King, Judge, Redeemer, the Lord Our Righteousness. Other titles He and God shared were Light, Rock, Husband, Shepherd, Creator, Giver of Life, Forgiver of Sins, and Healer.

If Jesus were God, then along with claiming names and titles that only God could bear, He would also have to have attributes that only God could possess. Did He? Does Scripture teach that He did?

Chapter 3

Jesus Christ Possesses
the Attributes of God

God is unique. Only He is uncreated. He is the creator and sustainer of the whole universe—the source of creation rather than a part of creation. We can see God's handiwork or imprint on created things, but His handiwork is not a part of God or the same as God Himself. For example, human beings are personal—we can think, decide, imagine, love. We are in the *image* of God, who is personal, but we are not God.

If Jesus Christ is truly God, then He must possess the attributes of God, not just mirror them. In this chapter we will examine five exclusive attributes of God and see that Jesus Christ possesses those attributes.

Omnipresence

God is "in" everything; all of God is everywhere present at each point in the universe. That is what being *omnipresent* means. But to believe that God is "in" everything does not mean that He "is" everything. By saying that God is everywhere at once, we are not saying that God is in everything in the Hindu sense that all creation is in some way a part of God. For example, although God made the trees, a tree is not a part of God.[1]

Just as God is omnipresent in a personal sense (Psalm

51

139:7; Proverbs 15:3), and thus is able to help, deliver, love, defend, and meet His people's deepest longings and needs, so the New Testament describes Christ also as omnipresent. Paul said that *"He* who descended is *Himself* also *He* who ascended far above all the heavens, that *He might fill all things"* (Ephesians 4:10). Christ told His disciples, "For where two or three have gathered together in My Name, there I am in their midst" (Matthew 18:20). He told them, "Lo, I am with you always, even to the end of the age" (Matthew 28:20). Christ is said to indwell the hearts of all who place their faith in Him (Romans 8:9, Galatians 2:20, Ephesians 3:17, Colossians 1:27, Revelation 3:20). ". . . do you not recognize this about yourselves, that *Jesus Christ is in you?"* (2 Corinthians 13:5). How could a mere mortal, glorified or not, claim to indwell the hearts of believers around the world?

Omniscience

When we say that God is *omniscient,* we mean that God knows everything that can be known, actual and potential, throughout eternity.

God has a perfect and eternal knowledge of all things. Everything that is able to be known, is known by God. The omniscience of God does not come in the same way that knowledge comes to [us]. We arrive at knowledge by learning. God does not go through the learning process to know. The omniscience of God does not come through reasoning, inference, the senses, imagination, or induction or deduction. His knowledge is direct, sharp and distinct, true to the reality of things. Whatever can be known, is known, by God.[2]

The New Testament pictures Christ as possessing omniscience: cognizance of all—past, present, and future. In John 2:24,25 it is stated that Jesus "knew all men" and "knew what was in man." The disciples bore witness, "Now we know that You know all things" (John 16:30). Peter declared, "Lord, You know all things" (John 21:17). In keeping with His omniscience, Christ was said to have foreknown those who would betray Him (John 6:64).

Speaking of Christ's omniscience, Dr. John Walvoord states:

In a similar way Christ's foreknowledge is affirmed in other passages (John 13:1, 11; 18:4; 19:28). In keeping with His omniscience, He is declared to have the wisdom of God (1 Corinthians 1:30). Such qualities could not be ascribed to even the wisest of prophets, and they constitute another proof that He possessed all of the divine attributes.[3]

Thomas Schultz observes that:

The knowledge of Christ is far beyond any mortal knowledge. He is not just a genius, not just the wisest of all humans. His wisdom far exceeds all human limitations and could only be classified as perfect knowledge. First, He knows the inward thoughts and memories of man, an ability peculiar to God (1 Kings 8:39; Jeremiah 17:9-16). He saw the evil in the hearts of the scribes (Matthew 9:4); He knew beforehand those who would reject Him (John 10:64) and those who would follow Him (John 10:14). He could read the hearts of every man and woman (Mark 2:8; John 1:48; 2:24, 25; 4:16-19; Acts 1:24; 1 Corinthians 4:5; Revelation 2:18-23). A mere human can no more than make an intelligent guess as to what is in the hearts and minds of others. Second, Christ has a knowledge of other facts beyond the possible comprehension of any man. He knew just where the fish were in the water (Luke 5:4-6; John 21:6-11), and He knew just which fish contained the coin (Matthew 17:27). He knew future events (John 11:11; 18:4), details that would be encountered (Matthew 21:2-4), and He knew that Lazarus had died (John 11:14). Third, He possessed an inner knowledge of the Godhead showing the closest possible communion with God as well as perfect knowledge. He knows the Father as the Father knows Him (Matthew 11:27; John 7:29; 8:55; 10:15; 17:25). The fourth and consummating teaching of Scripture along this line is that Christ knows all things (John 16:30; 21:17), and that in Him are hidden all the treasures of wisdom and knowledge (Colossians 2:3).[4]

Omnipotence

The Hebrew words *El Shaddai* can be translated "God Almighty." God is *omnipotent* or all-powerful. Christ's miracles evidenced His power over the physical world. But His words and His resurrection proclaim an authority and power over all creation.

Dr. John Walvoord has written:

The evidence for the omnipotence of Christ is as decisive as proof for other attributes. Sometimes it takes the form of physical power, but more often it refers to authority over creation. Christ has the power to forgive sins (Matt. 9:6), all power in heaven and in earth (Matt. 28:18), power over nature (Luke 8:25), power over His own life (John 10:18), power to give eternal life to others (John 17:2), power to heal physically, as witnessed by His many miracles, as well as power to cast out demons (Mark 1:29-34), and power to transform the body (Phil. 3:21). By virtue of His resurrection "He is able also to save them to the uttermost that come unto God by Him" (Heb. 7:25). He is "able to keep that which I have committed unto you against that day" (2 Tim. 1:12). He is "able to keep you from falling, and to present you faultless before the presence of His glory with exceeding joy" (Jude 24; cf. Eph. 5:27). The Greek text of Jude 25 seems to imply that this is "through Jesus Christ our Lord," that is, by God the Father; but in any case the power of Christ is needed. It will be observed that the incarnation, death and resurrection of Christ permitted Christ to act in regard to sin and salvation. His omnipotence in any case is restricted to that which is holy, wise and good.[5]

Pre-existence

Another attribute that Jesus and God share is pre-existence. Many passages in Scripture support Jesus' existing prior to His birth, not as a mere idea in the foreknowledge of God, but in actuality.

Jesus said, "I came forth *from* the Father, and have *come into the world;* I am leaving the world *again,* and going to the Father" (John 16:28). Many times Jesus said that He had been "sent" into the world, implying that His origin had been outside the world (John 3:32-34; 4:34; 5:23, 24, 36-38; 6:29, 33, 38; 7:16, 18, 28, 29, 33; 8:18, 29, 38, 42; 13:20; 16:30; 17:8, etc.) He told Nicodemus, ". . . no one has ascended into heaven, but He who *descended* from heaven, even the Son of Man" (John 3:13). He said, "I am [*ego eimi*] the living bread that *came down out of heaven* . . ." (John 6:51; see also v.58). Jesus said, "What then if you should behold the Son of Man ascending where He was *before*?" (John 6:62). John the Baptist said concerning Christ, "He who *comes from heaven* [Jesus] is above all. What He has *seen* and *heard,* of that He bears witness..." (John 3:31, 32).

On another occasion Jesus prayed, "... glorify Thou Me... with the glory which *I ever had with Thee before the world was*" (John 17:5). The writer of Hebrews assumed the pre-existence of Christ when he wrote that Moses considered the "reproach of Christ greater riches than the treasures of Egypt" (Hebrews 11:26). Jesus is said to have possessed the "book of life" from the "foundation of the world" (Revelation 13:8).

John the Baptist, who was humanly six months older than Jesus, said, "He who comes after me has a higher rank than I, for *He existed before me*" (John 1:15, 30). Verse 30 clearly shows that John was referring to Jesus, not "God." John the Baptist could not have been referring to Jesus' existing in the foreknowledge of God either, as some believe, since God, who is all-knowing, would have foreknown John too.

Thus Scripture speaks with a unified voice. Jesus is a pre-existent being. This is in keeping with Old Testament theophanies (that is, times when God appeared in a physical form). For example, Genesis 18:1—19:1; 16:7-13; 22:15, 16; 31:11-13; 32:30; 48:15, 16; Exodus 4:2-4 (cf. 3:2); 1 Chronicles 21:15-19; Psalm 34:6, 7; Zechariah 12:10 (cf. John 19:37); and 14:3, 4 (cf. Acts 1:9-12) are a few of the main passages showing that God has appeared physically.[6]

Eternalness

The God of the Bible is *eternal.* He is both beyond time

and the source of time. There was never a time when He was not: there never will be a time when He is not (Exodus 3:14; Habakkuk 3:6; Deuteronomy 33:26, 27). Only God is eternal.

Jesus Christ is also eternal. He did not have a "beginning," as the Jehovah's Witnesses and members of The Way International assert (and even, in a sense, also the Mormons).

In foretelling the birth of Jesus the Messiah, the prophet Micah said, "His goings forth are from long ago, from the days of eternity" (Micah 5:2). Isaiah, also speaking of Christ's birth, said that among other designations, the child would be called "*Eternal* Father" (Isaiah 9:6). Jesus said, "Before Abraham was born, I AM" (John 8:58). The Greek text clearly uses the present tense, "I am," not "I was." F. F. Bruce points out, "Had he been merely a pre-existent being then He would have had to say, 'Before Abraham was I was.'"[7] Jesus went a long step further, speaking of Himself as the eternal, ever-present "I AM."

G. Campbell Morgan has stated, "'I AM' claims the eternity of existence, antedating the whole of the Hebrew economy, existing in eternal Being."[8]

William Barclay's comment is also important:

> Jesus is *timeless*. There never was a time when He came into being; there never will be a time when He is not in being. We cannot say of Jesus, *He was*. We must always say, "He is." . . . in Jesus we see the timeless God, who was the God of Abraham and of Isaac and of Jacob, who was before time and who will be after time, who always *is*.[9]

Immutability

Webster's Dictionary defines immutability as "not being

capable of or susceptible to change." God is *immutable* in His person. Although He acts in time, and establishes and changes relationships in time, His essence, which includes his attributes, never changes (Malachi 3:6; James 1:17; Psalm 33:11; Isaiah 46:9, 10). We can rely on Him to love us eternally and keep His promises. Jesus obviously went through human developmental changes. Yet, concerning His divine nature, Scripture boldly asserts that "Jesus Christ is the same yesterday and today, yes and forever" (Hebrews 13:8). Jesus and the Father stand as immutably one in essence.

Thus we see how many verses in Scripture reveal that Jesus Christ possesses all of the attributes of the eternal God.

Chapter 4

Jesus Christ Possesses
the Authority of God

The authority of God in Jesus is seen in Christ taking upon Himself the right to be worshiped. He also claimed authority to resurrect Himself, and He spoke with an awesome authority, as God Himself.

Received Worship

Few subjects are spoken of in Scripture with more clarity than the subject of worship. Both the Old and New Testaments emphasize that God alone should receive worship. Jesus told Satan, "You shall worship the Lord your God, and serve Him only" (Matthew 4:10; Luke 4:8). No man or angel was ever to receive worship (Matthew 4:10; Revelation 19:20; 22:8, 9). God would not give his "glory" to another (Isaiah 42:8).

The New Testament uses one word primarily for worship, the Greek word *proskuneo.* It is the word Jesus used in telling Satan to worship God alone; it is used more than any other word in describing worship of God (John 4:24; Revelation 5:14; 7:11; 11:16; etc.).

After Jesus healed a man, the person exclaimed, "'Lord I believe!' And he worshiped [past tense form of *proskuneo*] Him" (John 9:38). The same Greek word is used in Matthew 14:33, when the disciples worshiped Jesus after seeing

Him walk on water. Another time the disciples, seeing Jesus after the resurrection, "came up and took hold of His feet and worshiped him" (Matthew 28:9). Thus, before and after the resurrection, Jesus received worship. In all of those instances, the same Jesus who had rebuked Satan for tempting Him to worship wrongly did not recoil in horror because "Only God is to be worshiped." Instead, He received the worship as His due.

In Hebrews 1:6 the angels of God are told to worship (*proskuneo*) Jesus. In Revelation 5:8-14, a whole section of praise and worship is devoted to Jesus the "Lamb" and to God. In a powerful passage, Paul stated that at the name of Jesus every knee in heaven and earth will bow (implying worship) and confess that Jesus is Lord (Philippians 2:10, 11). The Son of God was worshiped through numerous acts in the New Testament as He became the object of faith, hope, and adoration.

The united testimony of the New Testament church and, indeed, of the church throughout all centuries, is that worship is due to the Triune God: Father, Son, and Holy Spirit.

Had Authority to Resurrect Himself

Even while Jesus was subject to death as a man, He claimed the power and authority to resurrect Himself, a power only God could have. Some people might ask, "If Jesus Christ is God, how could He resurrect Himself?" In John 2:19 Jesus said, "Destroy this temple [referring to his body—v. 21], and in three days *I will raise it up.*" Concerning His life He said, "I have authority to lay it down, and I have authority to take it up again" (John 10:18).

Spoke as God

Not only did Jesus claim the names, titles, and attributes of God, receive worship, and claim the authority to resurrect Himself, but He also spoke things that only God could rightfully speak. Once when the Pharisees had sent officers to arrest Him, the officers returned empty-handed. When asked why they had not arrested Him, all they could reply was, "Never did a man speak the way this man speaks" (John 7:46). It was true.

It is difficult to read the Gospel narratives without being struck by Jesus' divine authority. He called people to Himself, asking them to follow Him even to the extent of laying down their lives. He spoke with a personal authority unique in the experience of His audience. Other teachers of His day, the scribes and Pharisees, quoted the law and the prophets to substantiate their points. Jesus said, "Truly, truly, I say . . ." Events affirmed His authority. Demons fled at His word. Wind and sea stilled at His command. The dead rose, the crippled walked, the blind saw. C. S. Lewis wrote,

A man who was merely a man and said the sort of things Jesus said would not be a great moral teacher. He would either be a lunatic—on a level with the man who says he is a poached egg—or else the Devil of Hell. You must make your choice. Either this man was, and is, the Son of God: or else a madman or something worse. You can shut him up for a fool, you can spit at him and kill him as a demon, or you can fall at his feet and call him Lord and God. But let us not come with any patronizing nonsense about his being a great moral teacher. He has not left that open to us. He did not intend to.[1]

Scriptural Glossary of Names, Titles, and Attributes Demonstrating That Jesus and Yahweh Are One
"There is one God"—1 Corinthians 8:6

Description	As Used of God	As Used of Jesus
YHWH (I AM)	Exodus 3:14 Deuteronomy 32:39 Isaiah 43:10	John 8:24 John 8:58 John 18:4-6
God	Genesis 1:1 Deuteronomy 6:4 Psalm 45:6,7	Isaiah 7:14, 9:6 John 1:1, 14 John 20:28 Titus 2:13 Hebrews 1:8 2 Peter 1:1
Alpha and Omega (First and Last)	Isaiah 41:4 Isaiah 48:12 Revelation 1:8	Revelation 1:17, 18 Revelation 2:8 Revelation 22:12-16
Lord	Isaiah 45:23	Matthew 12:8 Acts 7:59, 60 Acts 10:36 Romans 10:12 1 Corinthians 2:8 1 Corinthians 12:3 Philippians 2:10, 11
Savior	Isaiah 43:3 Isaiah 43:11 Isaiah 63:8 Luke 1:47 1 Timothy 4:10	Matthew 1:21 Luke 2:11 John 1:29 John 4:42 Titus 2:13 Hebrews 5:9
King	Psalm 95:3 Isaiah 43:15 1 Timothy 6:14-16	Revelation 17:14 Revelation 19:16

Judge	Genesis 18:25	John 5:22
	Psalm 50:4, 6	2 Corinthians 5:10
	Psalm 96:13	2 Timothy 4:1
	Romans 14:10	
Light	2 Samuel 22:29	John 1:4, 9
	Psalm 27:1	John 3:19
	Isaiah 42:6	John 8:12
		John 9:5
Rock	Deuteronomy 32:3, 4	Romans 9:33
	2 Samuel 22:32	1 Corinthians 10:3, 4
	Psalm 89:26	1 Peter 2:4-8
Redeemer	Psalm 130:7, 8	Acts 20:28
	Isaiah 48:17	Ephesians 1:7
	Isaiah 54:5	Hebrews 9:12
	Isaiah 63:9	
Our Righteousness	Isaiah 45:24	Jeremiah 23:6
		Romans 3:21-22
Husband	Isaiah 54:5	Matthew 25:1
	Hosea 2:16	Mark 2:18, 19
		(Bridegroom)
		2 Corinthians 11:2
		Ephesians 5:25-32
		Revelation 21:2, 9
Shepherd	Genesis 49:24	John 10:11, 16
	Psalm 23:1	Hebrews 13:20
	Psalm 80:1	1 Peter 2:25
		1 Peter 5:4
Creator	Genesis 1:1	John 1:2, 3, 10
	Job 33:4	Colossians 1:15-18
	Psalm 95:5, 6	Hebrews 1:1-3, 10
	Psalm 102:25, 26	
	Isaiah 40:28	
Giver of Life	Genesis 2:7	John 5:21
	Deuteronomy 32:39	John 10:28
	1 Samuel 2:6	John 11:25
	Psalm 36:9	

Forgiver of Sin	Exodus 34:6-7	Mark 2:1-12
	Nehemiah 9:17	Acts 26:18
	Daniel 9:9	Colossians 2:13
	Jonah 4:2	Colossians 3:13
Lord Our Healer	Exodus 15:26	Acts 9:34
Omnipresent	Psalm 139:7-12	Matthew 18:20
	Proverbs 15:3	Matthew 28:20
		Ephesians 3:17; 4:10
Omniscient	1 Kings 8:39	Matthew 11:27
	Jeremiah 17:9, 10, 16	Luke 5:4-6
		John 2:25
		John 16:30
		John 21:17
		Acts 1:24
Omnipotent	Isaiah 40:10-31, 18	Matthew 28:18
	Isaiah 45:5-13, 18	Mark 1:29-34
		John 10:18
		Jude 24
Pre-Existent	Genesis 1:1	John 1:15, 30
		John 3:13, 31, 32
		John 6:62
		John 16:28
		John 17:5
Eternal	Psalm 102:26, 27	Isaiah 9:6
	Habakkuk 3:6	Micah 5:2
		John 8:58
Immutable	Isaiah 46:9, 16	Hebrews 13:8
	Malachi 3:6	
	James 1:17	
Receiver of Worship	Matthew 4:10	Matthew 14:33
	John 4:24	Matthew 28:9
	Revelation 5:14	John 9:38
	Revelation 7:11	Philippians 2:10, 11
	Revelation 11:16	Hebrews 1:6
Speaker with Divine Authority	"Thus saith the Lord..."—used hundreds of times	Matthew 23:34-37
		John 7:46
		"Truly, truly, I say...."

Chapter 5

God Became Man in Jesus Christ

The Scriptures teach that Jesus was fully God while also being fully human. Paul declared of Jesus, "For in Him all the fulness of deity dwells in bodily form" (Colossians 2:9). Because Jesus is both fully God and fully man, He stands in a unique relationship in the Trinity to the Father and the Holy Spirit.

At the incarnation Jesus chose voluntarily to put Himself under the Father's authority. He did that not because He had to, but because He chose to, as part of God's plan. Paul explained this in Philippians 2:5-8:

> Have this attitude in yourselves which was also in Christ Jesus, who, although *He existed in the form of God,* did not regard equality with God a thing to be grasped, but emptied Himself, *taking the form of a bond-servant,* and being made in the likeness of men. And *being found in appearance as a man,* He humbled Himself by becoming obedient to the point of death, even death on a cross.

The statement that Jesus gave up His equality with God assumes that He had equality to begin with. (The Greek word here for "equality" comes from the root word *isos,* used in geometry to describe the isosceles triangle with its two equal sides.)

The Philippians passage also teaches that Jesus "existed"

in two forms: as God (v.6) and then as a bond servant (v.7), "being found in appearance as a man." The fact that Paul mentioned that Jesus was found in appearance as a man indicates that it was the unexpected— God become man. The word *grasped* does not imply that Jesus was grasping after equality with God, but rather, having equality, He did not grasp or hold on to His divine prerogatives while on earth. He lived His earthly life by the power of His Father. God the Son, in submission (by rank, not by nature) to God the Father, became man, took on a second real nature, a human nature, and then voluntarily performed the ultimate act of submission: sacrifice of Himself for the sins of the world.

Jesus' submission does not deny His essential equality with the Father and the Holy Spirit. God's Son must be of the same nature as His Father. This is illustrated in John 5:17, 18 and is explained by biblical commentator Leon Morris:

> . . . we read that Jesus on a sabbath day cured a lame man in Jerusalem and that He came into violent conflict with the Jewish leaders as a result. Jesus' defense was, 'My Father worketh even until now, and I work' (John 5:17). The Jews were enraged 'because he not only broke the sabbath, but also called God his own Father, making himself equal with God' (v.18). . . The imperfect tense denotes not a single, isolated happening, but a continuing practice. Moreover this practice was not aimless, nor due to religious carelessness or the like. It proceeded from Jesus' idea of His relationship to the heavenly Father. It was because He was the Son that He acted as He did on the sabbath. Therefore the Jews saw in His attitude to the sabbath not merely the breaking of one of the commandments, but blasphemy, and that of the most serious kind: 'making himself equal with God.' Small wonder that they persecuted Him in Galilee.[1]

Just as the Father was continually working (the implication being that of sustaining the universe, etc.) Jesus said that He too was working—not as a servant obeying the Father, but on a par with the Father. As Professor E. W. Hengstenberg states:

> The proposition that God works unceasingly, on the Sabbath not less than on the other days, was common to the Jews of Christ. The rest on the seventh day in Genesis 2:3, as is expressly remarked, refers only to the creative work, and was always so referred by the Jews. It pertained only to the first Sabbath. The later Divine operation knows no distinction of days. That Christ called God His Father in a different sense from that in which He was so called by all Israel (Isaiah 54:7), was implied, as the Jews perceived, in the conclusion which He drew from this relation.[2]

Jesus' point is that just as the Father works, so the Son works. His choice of words was no accident. The sabbath was meant for rest, not working, and Jesus had just healed someone on the sabbath. But Jesus went on to state that both He and the Father, His own unique Father, were working. As the Father continually sustains His creation, so too Jesus continually sustains the creation (see also Colossians 1:16). To the Jew this was blasphemy.

The Jews understood what Jesus was saying by calling God His *own* Father. Jesus was not claiming, as the Jews often did, that God was "our Father" in a covenant sense. Rather, Jesus claimed a special, unique, and natural relationship to the Father when He referred to God as "my Father."

C. K. Barrett comments:

> Jesus had called God his own father . . . a form of speech which did not arise out of liturgical custom or the notion

of Israel as God's child . . . and the assumption of a uniform activity common to Jesus and to God could mean only that Jesus was equal to God.[3]

Because Jesus took on human form in the incarnation, we can see God *in the fullest sense possible in this world.* In Jesus Christ, the God-man, we behold the "glory as of the only begotten" (John 1:14). Yet other passages say, "no man can see Me [God] and live," "no man has seen God at any time," "whom no man has seen or can see" (referring to God) (Exodus 33:20; John 1:18; 1 Timothy 6:16; 1 John 4:12, etc.).

No one could see the totality of God in all His power and splendor and live—that is true. Even the presence of angelic beings caused godly individuals overwhelming fear and awe, almost to the point of death (Daniel 10:5-11).

Yet God has been "seen." When Moses asked to see God, God replied, "No man can see Me and live." But, God went on, He would place Moses in the cleft of the rock and put His hand over him. Then His "glory" would pass by. After His glory passed, God said, "Then I will take My hand away and you shall see My back, but My face shall not be seen" (Exodus 33:23). So Moses saw God, though only to a degree he could handle. There are other instances, too, in which God has been "seen." After Jacob had wrestled with a "man," a physical manifestation of God, Scripture says he had "striven with God" (Genesis 32:28 compare Hosea 12:3-4). Jacob said, "I have seen God face to face, yet my life has been preserved" (Genesis 32:30). Moses, Aaron, Nadab, and Abihu, along with seventy elders of Israel, "saw the God of Israel . . . and they beheld God" (Exodus 24:9-11). Samson's father exclaimed, "We shall surely die, for we have seen God" (Judges 13:22). After a heavenly vision of God, Isaiah said, "I saw the Lord . . . my eyes have seen the King, the Lord of hosts" (Isaiah 6:1-3, 5).

So the picture Scripture gives is that human beings cannot see the total glory and power of God and live. Yet God has been "seen" to the degree that our earthly capacities could perceive Him.

The New Testament teaches that God has been seen in time and history in the person of Jesus Christ. Jesus said that to see Him was the same as seeing God (John 12:45; 14:5-9). Colossians 1:15 says that Christ is the "image of the invisible God." The writer of Hebrews wrote that Christ is the "radiance of His [the Father's] glory and the exact representation of His nature" (Hebrews 1:3). The Greek means "exact reproduction," a stronger term than in Colossians 1:15. According to Joseph H. Thayer, it was used for the impression produced by a seal or a die stamp in wax or metal, i.e., an exact impression, a "precise reproduction in every respect."[4]

The revelation of God in Christ is a foretaste of the coming full revelation of the Holy Trinity. Jesus Christ came first to beckon and entreat. He is coming again to judge and demand. As C. S. Lewis expressed it:

Why is God landing in this enemy occupied world in disguise and starting a sort of secret society to undermine the devil? Why is He not landing in force, invading it? Is it that He is not strong enough? Well, Christians think He is going to land in force; we do not know when. But we can guess why He is delaying. He wants to give us the chance of joining His side freely. I do not suppose you and I would have thought much of a Frenchman who waited till the Allies were marching into Germany and then announced he was on our side. God will invade. But I wonder whether people who ask God to interfere openly and directly in our world quite realize what it will be like when He does. When that happens, it is the end of the world. When the author walks on to the stage the play is over. God is going to invade, all right; but what is the good of saying you are on His side then, when you see the whole natural universe melting away like a dream and something else—something it never entered your head to conceive—comes crashing in; something so beautiful to some of us and so terrible to others that none of us will have any choice left? For this time it will be God without disguise; something so overwhelming that it will strike either irresistible love or irresistible horror into every creature. It will be too late then to choose your side.[5]

Jesus Christ as Son

In the Bible, the word *son* is used several ways, generically or figuratively. In Greek, two words were translated "son": *teknon* and *huios. Teknon,* the Greek equivalent of our word *son,* came from a root word having to do with childbearing and could be translated son, daughter, or child. The other Greek word, *huios,* could also be used literally; but as *Strong's Exhaustive Concordance* indicates, was "used very widely of immediate or figurative kinship."[6]

The word *Son* was used of Jesus in at least four ways: Son of Mary, Son of David, Son of Man, Son of God. Those four terms together describe the natural relationship of Jesus to the Father and to humankind.

Son of Mary. According to His human nature, Jesus had one parent, Mary. In this sense, Jesus of Nazareth was literally and physically a "son."

Son of David. In this instance, Son (*huios*) of David is often looked at as figurative because Jesus was not a literal first generation descendant of David (see Matthew 22:42-45). However, it also can mean that Jesus is a descendant and heir of David.

Son of Man. The term *son of man* is distinctly Jewish and is first used in the Old Testament. Two words were used

for *man*—*adam* and *nos*—and both were used in the col-
lective sense (i.e., humankind). An individual might be
called "a son of man." The prophet Ezekiel, for example,
was referred to ninety times as "son of man." The phrase
seemed to take on messianic overtones in Daniel 7:13, 14.

In the New Testament the term "Son of Man" was used
exclusively of Jesus, except in Hebrews 2:6-8 where it is
used for humankind generally. Whereas the Old Testament
used it in a general sense, Jesus used it as a figurative title,
saying He was "*the* Son of Man." Only three times is the
phrase used of Jesus outside the Gospels (Acts 7:56; Revelation 1:13; 14:14). It is used thirty-two times in Matthew,
fifteen times in Mark, twenty-five times in Luke, and twelve
times in John; and in each case came from the lips of Jesus
Himself (except John 12:34, when someone asked Him
what he meant by the title).

The frequent use of the term appears in every facet of
Christ's life: His public ministry, suffering, and future glori-
fication.[7] Throughout the Gospels, Jesus continually gave
fuller meaning to the title.

Christ's use of the title seems to run along two lines of
thought. First, the use of Son of Man reveals a divine figure.
Christ used the phrase to demonstrate His authority to
forgive sin (Matthew 9:6; Mark 2:10; Luke 5:24) and His
being the Lord of the sabbath (Matthew 12:8; Mark 2:28;
Luke 6:5). The emphasis is on Christ's authority. (The clear
indication is that Christ claims authority possessed only
by God. This emphasis on the divine can also be seen in
Christ's use of the term with regard to His future glori-
fication.)

Second, the use of the term Son of Man reveals a human
figure. Without question Christ's use of the title is often
indicative of His desire to point to His manhood as well as
to His divinity. We see that in two significant ways in the
Gospels: first, the title is used of Christ as He goes about

what might be called His daily work (Matthew 11:19). Second, the title is used of Jesus concerning His suffering and death (Mark 8:31). The very idea of Jesus being human foreshadows the fact that He must eventually die, a concept the Jews had difficulty believing would be true of their Messiah. Third, Jesus not only presented Himself as the Son of Man who had to suffer and die, but also as the one who was going to return to glory (Matthew 24:30; Mark 14:62; Luke 17:22; 18:8; 22:69, etc.).

At His trial before the Sanhedrin and the high priest Caiaphas, He clearly identified Himself as the "Son of Man" referred to in Daniel 7:13, 14.

> I kept looking in the night visions, and behold, with the clouds of heaven One like a Son of Man was coming, and He came up to the Ancient of Days and was presented before Him. And to Him was given dominion, glory and a kingdom that all the peoples, nations, and men of every language might serve Him . . .

Caiaphas asked Jesus, "'Are you the Christ, the Son of the Blessed One [God]?' And Jesus said, "I am [ego eimi]; and you shall see the Son of Man sitting at the right hand of Power and coming with the clouds of heaven'" (Mark 14:61-62). Saying that, Jesus made a powerful assertion about His coming return with great glory to judge and rule over the earth. In that encounter with Caiaphas it is significant that Jesus accepted simultaneously the titles "Son of Man" and "Son of the Blessed One" (compare John 3:15-17).

Gleason Archer explains why the Messiah would of necessity have two natures, human and divine:

This raises the question of what the title "Son of Man"... signified. Why was the Messiah represented as a glorified human being rather than as the divine King of Glory? The answer is to be found in the necessity of the Incarnation as indispensable to man's redemption. The fallen, guilty race of Adam could not have their sins atoned for except by a Sin-Bearer who represented them as a true human being as He laid down His life for their sake. The Old Testament term for Redeemer is *go el,* which implies "kinsman-redeemer." He therefore had to be related by blood to the person whose cause he took over and whose need he supplied, whatever it was, whether to buy him back from slavery (Leviticus 25:48), to redeem his forfeited property foreclosed on a mortgage (Leviticus 25:25), to care for his childless widow (Ruth 3:13), or to avenge his blood on the murderer (Numbers 35:19).

God revealed Himself to Israel as *go el* of His covenant people (Exodus 6:6; 15:13; Isaiah 43:1; Psalm 19:14...); but before God became Man by the miracle of the Incarnation and the Virgin Birth, it was a mystery to God's ancient people how He could ever qualify as their *go el.* God was their Father by creation, to be sure, but *go el* implies a blood relationship on a physical level. And so God had to become one of us in order to redeem us from the guilt and penalty of our sin. "And the Word became flesh, and dwelt among us, and we beheld His glory, glory as of the only begotten from the Father, full of grace and truth" (John 1:14).

God as God could not forgive us for our sins unless our sins were fully paid for; otherwise He would have been a condoner and protector of the violation of His own holy law. It was only as a man that God in Christ could furnish satisfaction sufficient to atone for the sins of mankind; for only a man, a true human being, could properly represent the human race. But our Redeemer had to be God, for only God could furnish a sacrifice of infinite value, to compensate for the penalty of eternal hell that our sin demands, according to the righteous claims of divine justice. Only God could have devised a way of salvation that made it possible for Him to remain just and at the same time become the Justifier of the ungodly (Romans 4:5), instead of sending them to the everlasting perdition they deserved . . . for it was the perfect Man who was also infinite God that furnished an effectual sacrifice for all believers of every age.[8]

Christ's use of the term "Son of Man" takes on its fullest implications when one considers the Daniel 7:13 reference. The title is undeniably messianic, and Christ clearly claimed to be the one referred to by Daniel 7:13. The title in Daniel seems to have been understood by the Jews as messianic, but the two assertions added by Jesus were not counted on by the Jewish leaders. First, the Jews saw a conquering Messiah in the prophetic forecast, not a suffering one. Their emphasis was more on a political than spiritual deliverer. Yet Jesus portrayed the Son of Man as a suffering Messiah, one who must come to die. Second, the Jewish leaders had not looked to the Messiah's being God incarnate. Traditionally, it was one thing to claim Messiahship but it was something entirely different to claim to be a divine Messiah.

In summary, the title "Son of Man," an obscure term to Jesus' contemporaries, was laden with insights into the nature of the Messiah as kinsman-redeemer, suffering servant, and coming judge and world ruler.

Son of God

We now come to the phrase, "Son of God." How are we to understand it? That Jesus Christ is the Son of God, the second person of the Holy Trinity, is essential to the doctrine of the incarnation. Jesus is the Son of God in Scripture. The Father did not become man. The Spirit did not become man. The Son became man. Some people have questions about the word *Son,* interpreting it, wherever it appears, in the literal sense, as a son is born to a father and mother. According to their reasoning, there is no way Jesus could be God because he was God's son. Some people, using the fact that Jesus is a son, might say, "Did you ever hear of a son who did not have a beginning?" By this they mean to contrast the "created" son with the uncreated Father. Of course, the question may be turned around, "Did you ever hear of a father who didn't have a beginning?" The term "Son [*huios*] of God" can be used to imply the full deity of Christ just as the term "Son of Man," as discussed earlier, implied His full humanity (and deity).

Son of Man = Full Humanity (and Deity)

Son of God = Full Deity

W.G.T. Shedd states, "the denomination 'Son,' given to the second trinitarian person, denotes an Immanent and eternal relation of the essence."[9] An obvious implication of Shedd's point is that if the Father is eternal, then so is the Son. As Schultz points out, "Christ's sonship and the First Person's fatherhood do not connote inferiority either of essence or position."[10]

Boettner makes a key point:

> In connection with an earlier treatment of the doctrine of the Trinity we have pointed out that in theological language the terms "Father" and "Son" carry with them not our occidental ideas of, on the one hand, source of being and superiority, and on the other, subordination and dependence, but rather the Semitic and oriental ideas of

likeness or *sameness of nature* and equality of being. It is, of course, the Semitic consciousness that underlies the phraseology of Scriptures, and whenever the Scriptures call Christ the "Son of God" they assert His true and proper Deity. It signifies a unique relationship that cannot be predicated of nor shared with any creature. As any merely human son is like his father in his essential nature, that is, possessed of humanity, so Christ, the Son of God, was like His Father in His essential nature, that is, possessed of Deity.[11]

Schultz elaborates:

Although others in Scripture are called "sons of God," for example, angels, Adam, Ezekiel, and Christians, Christ is the Son in a unique and exclusive sense. Griffith Thomas carefully notes that the title "Son of God" is found in these forms in the Greek—sometimes with the article before each of the two words, sometimes with the article omitted altogether. The first of these forms, at least, is a title of deity and is found twenty-five times in the New Testament applied to Christ. By this title the Jews understood the high claims of Christ and condemned Him because of its meaning and implications (Matthew 26:63; Luke 22:70; John 19:7). It was a claim to deity and not merely to Messiahship. The Lord never classified His sonship with the sonship of others. He actually went into detail to keep the two distinct and separate (John 20:17). The disciples understood that Christ as the Son of God was the eternal God.[12]

What becomes evident is that the various uses of the title point to the truth of the Incarnation—that *God* became a *man*. If the term Son of Man means that Christ is man, the term Son of God means that Christ is God.

Chapter 6

We Have the Witness
of the Early Church

The witness of the early Christian church is clear in its support of Christ's deity. The writings of the church fathers and apologists, accessible in translation today, proved their belief in this paramount doctrine.

The church fathers refer to Christ as being "eternal," "God incarnate," "creator," or possessing some other exclusive divine attribute in their writings.[1] Representative quotes from several of them follow:

• *Polycarp* (A.D. 69-155), bishop of Smyrna, was a disciple of the apostle John. He wrote: "Now may the God and Father of our Lord Jesus Christ, and the *eternal* High Priest Himself, the [Son of] God Jesus Christ, build you up in faith . . ."[2]

• *Ignatius* (died c. A.D. 110), head of the church at Antioch, was a contemporary of Polycarp, Clement, and Barnabas, and was martyred in the Colosseum. In his *Epistle to the Ephesians,* he wrote of Christ as "Our God, Jesus Christ."[3]

In another letter Ignatius admonished Polycarp to "await Him that is above every season, the *Eternal,* The *Invisible, who became visible for our sake . . .* who suffered for our sake."[4]

To the above he added in correspondence to the Smyrneans that " . . . if they believe not in the blood of Christ, (*who is God*), judgment awaiteth them also."[5]

The following excerpts are from Kirsopp Lake:[6]

77

Ignatius to the Ephesians i, greeting—". . . Jesus Christ our God. . ."

Ignatius to the Ephesians i.1—". . . by the blood of God. . ."

Ignatius to the Ephesians vii.2—". . . who is God in man. . ."

Ignatius to the Ephesians xvii.2—". . . received knowledge of God, that is, Jesus Christ"

Ignatius to the Ephesians xviii.2—"For our God, Jesus the Christ,. . ."

Ignatius to the Ephesians xix.3—". . . for God was manifest as man. . ."

Ignatius to the Magnesians xi.1—". . . Christ, who was from eternity with the Father. . ."

Ignatius to the Magnesians xiii.2—"Jesus Christ was subject to the Father."

Ignatius to the Trallians vii.1—". . . from God, from Jesus Christ. . ."

Ignatius to the Romans, greeting—"Jesus Christ, our God" (twice)

Ignatius to the Romans iii.3—". . . Our God, Jesus Christ."

Ignatius to the Romans vi.3—". . . suffer me to follow the example of the Passion of my God."

Ignatius to the Smyrneans i.1—Jesus Christ, the God

Ignatius to Polycarp viii.3—". . . our God, Jesus Christ."

Epistle of Barnabas vii.2—"Son of God, though he was the Lord. . ."

Researcher and author John Weldon has noted that the ". . . fact that Ignatius was not rebuked or branded as heretic by any of the people or churches he sent letters to shows that the early church, long before A.D. 115, universally accepted the deity of Christ."[7]

• *Irenaeus* (c. A.D. 125-200), a disciple of Polycarp, explained in *Against Heresi es* (4:10) how Christ was often seen by Moses and that it was Christ who spoke from the burning bush. Irenaeus continued elaborating on Christ's relationship to God the Father: "For with Him were always present the Word and Wisdom, the Son and the Spirit, *by whom* and in whom, freely and spontaneously, *He made all things,* to whom also He speaks, saying, 'Let us make man after our image and likeness.'"[8]

• *Justin Martyr* (A.D. 110-166), an apologist who defended the faith in a very scholarly manner, acknowledged, "I have often said, often enough, that when My God says, 'God went up from Abraham,' or 'the Lord spake unto Moses,' and 'the Lord came down to see the tower which the sons of men had built,' or 'God shut Noah within the Ark,' you must not imagine that the unbegotten God himself went down or went up anywhere. For the ineffable Father and Lord of all neither comes anywhere, nor walks, nor sleeps, nor rises up." Abraham and Isaac and Jacob saw not the ineffable Lord, but God, His Son, "who was also fire when He spoke with Moses from the bush" (*Dialogues,* cxxxvii). He continued: "Our Christ conversed with Moses under the appearance of fire from a bush." It was not the Father of the universe who thus spoke to Moses; but "Jesus the Christ," "the Angel and Apostle," "who is also God," yea "the God of Abraham, Isaac, and Jacob," and "the I am that I am" (*First Apology,* lxii; lxiii).

• *Clement* (died c. A.D. 101), bishop of Rome, in *Didache,* (chapter 16), applies to our Lord a quotation from Zechariah (14:5), "The Lord shall come and all the saints with Him"; and in the fourteenth chapter refers to Him two quotations loosely drawn from Malachi 1:11, 14, and likewise referring to Jehovah. *I Clement* presents "our Lord Jesus

Christ, the sceptre of the majesty of God" (xvi), as the Lord whom Malachi expected to come suddenly to His temple (xxiii); who had spoken through the Holy Ghost already in the Old Testament.

These are just a few of the many writings that could have been quoted from the church fathers.

Should anyone claim that these documents were forged, then the burden of proof rests on that person to substantiate his charges and produce historically documented writings of the early church saying that Christ was *not* God. After hundreds of years none has been found and authenticated as written by any church leader prior to Arius (early fourth century).

Second, concerning the argument that Scripture may have been tampered with, and significant doctrines added later, all of the New Testament as it is known today, with the exception of about eleven verses, can be found in the writings of the early church fathers *before* A.D. 325, not counting thousands of whole or partial Greek and Latin manuscripts of the New Testament which we possess. The Bible as it exists today is the most well-documented piece of ancient literature in the world. To delete all the verses that teach the divinity of Christ would leave the New Testament a tattered sham, a lie against all historical evidence.

The earliest record of a "Christian" denying the deity of Christ did not occur until A.D. 190, when a Byzantine leather merchant by the name of Theodotus, referring to his denial of Christ, said, "I have not denied God but a man . . ." Then it was not until A.D. 318-320, when a presbyter from Alexandria by the name of Arius denied the deity of Christ, that the question became a major theological issue within the church. The uproar that issue caused is strong evidence that the church, up to that time, had never seriously questioned the deity of Christ. Otherwise, Arius's teaching would have been ignored as commonplace. The beliefs Christians held at the time of the controversy, including their belief that Christ was God, had been formulated during two and a half centuries of severe persecution. The Council of Nicea (A.D. 325), was convened to resolve the issue ecclesiastically. After three months of painstaking deliberation, the deity of Christ was affirmed by that council. Arius and his two remaining supporters were expelled as heretics.[9]

Some argue that Constantine forced the orthodox view on those at the Council of Nicea, that out of fear the Christians succumbed to his wishes. That is not true. If anything, it was Constantine who was swayed by them. Historical records tell us that, upon seeing the scars and wounds of the believers who had been tortured for their faith in Christ, Constantine went around kissing those scars. These Christians, many of whom had lost eyes and limbs for their faith, would not have yielded to unholy pressure from Constantine.

Arius and his followers believed in the preexistence of Christ and that Christ was the creator of the world. The question of Jesus' being "only" a man was not an issue at the Council of Nicea; rather, the question was "Was Jesus 'God' or a 'god'?"

Despite his expulsion, Arius still swayed much of the church off and on for many years after the Council of Nicea. During that period, Athanasius, leader of the orthodox view and later bishop from Alexandria, was exiled five times by Arian leaders. Not until A.D. 381, at the Council of Constantinople, was the opposition permanently silenced.

The Nicene Creed, forged in turmoil and controversy, is still a theological cornerstone for the church.

Mark Noll writes of the Nicene Creed:

In **A.D.** 325 the Roman emperor, Constantine the Great, summoned leaders of the church to a little town across the Sea of Marmara from his new capital Constantinople [modern Istanbul]. Constantine was troubled by the religious dissension threatening the unity of his empire. The controversy focused on the teachings of a minor church official in Alexandria, Egypt. The bishops who met at Nicea to judge the teachings of this priest, Arius, produced a memorable confession of the Christian faith.

This confession, expanded by later additions, is known today as the Nicene Creed, a creed which was not only the first formal definition of the trinity against heretical teaching, but also the first Christian creed to gain universal acceptance in the church. (It is still used today in the worship services of the Orthodox, Roman Catholic, Lutheran, and Episcopal churches.) The importance of the creed lies in its forceful and unambiguous testimony of the unique nature of Jesus Christ as the savior of the world.

The doctrines which Arius taught illustrate the common tendency present throughout all of Christian history to subject the facts of God's revelation of himself in Christ and in Scripture to current conceptions of logic or "the reasonable." If, Arius argued, God (the Father) is absolutely perfect, absolutely transcendent, and absolutely without change, and if he is the originator of all things—without himself being derived from anything else—then it is obvious that everything and everyone else in the world is set apart from God. And, added Arius, if *everything* is set apart from God, then Jesus too must be set apart from God.

According to Arius, Jesus did play a special role in the creation and redemption of the physical world, but he was not himself God. There could be only one God; therefore, Christ must have been created at some time or another, Christ (like all the creation) must be subject to change and sin, and Christ (again, like all created beings) does not have real knowledge of the mind of God.

The council of Nicea, realizing how grave the threat was

which Arius's teaching posed to the Christian faith and yet how plausible its thin veneer of logic made it appear, constructed the following crucial assertions against Arius's thought:

(1) Christ was *very God of very God*. Jesus himself was God in the same sense in which the Father was God; any differentiation between Father and Son must refer to the respective task each does or to the relationship in which each stands to the other—but Father, Son and Spirit are all truly God.

(2) Christ was *of one substance with the Father*. The Greek word used in this phrase, *homoousios* (*homo* = "same," *ousios* = "substance"), led to great controversy, but it was chosen simply as a means of reinforcing as unequivocally as possible the fact that Christ was truly "very God of very God." It sought to summarize Jesus' own teaching: "I and the Father are one" (John 10:30).

(3) Christ was *begotten, not made*. That is, Christ was not created at any single point in time but was from eternity the Son of God.

(4) Christ became man *for us men and for our salvation*. The work of Christ was directed to the salvation of men, a salvation which could not have occurred if Christ were himself only a creature. Bluntly put, the Bible's teaching on the sinfulness of mankind indicated that the created realm was not able to pull itself to heaven by its own bootstraps. Salvation is of God.

The Nicene affirmation of faith faced much opposition. Many Arians refused to abandon their beliefs even when confronted by the creed's clear statement of Scriptural truth. The use of words not actually found in the Bible (like *homoousios*) bothered many Christians as did the fact that words like "substance" were often used ambiguously. But when Athanasius and other anti-Arians made it clear that "one substance" did not deny the separate person and work of Father, Son and Holy Spirit, the Creed gradually began to win acceptance.

The Nicene Creed is still today a hedge against that type of theological speculation which exalts human wisdom over God's revelation of Jesus Christ. It stands as an unambiguous distillation of Scripture's teaching concerning Christ's divine nature, his incarnation as a human being, and the work of salvation he accomplished for men. Finally, when the creed is used as a guide to Christian devotion or Christian proclamation, it can also become a vehicle through which the Holy Spirit transforms the truths of Christian faith into the realities of Christian life.

The Nicene Creed

I believe in one God the Father almighty, maker of heaven and earth, and of all things visible and invisible.

And in one Lord Jesus Christ, the only-begotten Son of God, begotten of the Father before all worlds, light of light, very God of very God, begotten, not made, being of one substance with the Father; by whom all things were made; who, for us men, and for our salvation, came down from heaven, and was incarnate by the Holy Ghost of the Virgin Mary, and was made man; and was crucified also for us under Pontius Pilate; he suffered and was buried; and the third day he rose again, according to the Scriptures; and ascended into heaven, and sits on the right hand of the Father; and he shall come again, with glory, to judge both the quick and the dead; whose kingdom shall have no end.

And in the Holy Spirit, the Lord and giver of life; who proceeds from the Father; who with the Father and the Son together is worshiped and glorified; who spoke by the prophets; and in one holy catholic and apostolic church. I confess one baptism for the remission of sins; and I look for the resurrection of the dead, and the life of the world to come. Amen. [Last paragraph added in A.D. 381].[10]

An article, "Deity of Christ," in the *Zondervan Pictorial Encyclopedia of the Bible,* states:

> The clearest and fullest expression of the deity of Christ is found in the Nicene Creed which was originally presented at the Council of Nicea, **A.D.** 325. In the *English Book of Common Prayer* the translation appears as follows: ". . . one Lord Jesus Christ, the only begotten Son of God, Light of Light, Very God of Very God, Begotten, not made." Set forth in this statement is every possible effort to make clear that Christ is "Very God of Very God." Closely allied with the word "deity" is the more general word "divinity." Deity is the stronger word, the absolute one. It can be argued that there is a "spark of divinity" in every man; not so with the word "deity."
>
> Only one person has ever made such claims for himself—Jesus Christ. His claims embrace the idea that what He teaches God Himself teaches, that what He has done only God could do, and that in His full personality there is an absolute oneness with God. To assert Himself in any way at all, is to assert God. Anyone making the claims for himself that Jesus Christ makes for Himself must be either mad and perverted or his claims must be true. Since the former simply cannot stand in the light of other evidence available, one is forced to conclude that the latter is established. Jesus Christ is what He claims to be: "Very God of Very God."[11]

Later, in 451, the Council of Chalcedon was convened. There the biblical doctrine of Jesus Christ as one divine person with two natures was formally delineated for the church. It is important to realize that those meetings of believers were not convened to sanction theological positions that were just emerging. Rather, they were convened to answer those opposed to the orthodox biblical position that was already held to be true.

It must also be remembered that, in those early days as the church expanded, there were no electronic media or jet-age transportation systems either to disseminate information or to insure accurate teaching. People depended on the communication of information by men and women of God who could get the word out accurately and effectively. The church councils served as a foundation for that process, facilitated by the presence of representatives from all of the major concentrations of Christians in the Roman world.

Thus, not only do the Scriptures bear testimony to Christ's divinity, but church history does that as well.

Chapter 7

What Are Some Common Objections to the Deity of Christ?

People today have a number of common objections to, or intellectual difficulties with, the issue of the deity of Christ. This chapter briefly discusses some of them, in particular some that arise among people who are quite familiar with biblical statements and phraseology. More extensive discussion can be found in books on the Recommended Reading List.

"The Father is Greater than I"

"Jesus said, '. . . the Father is greater than I' " (John 14:28). "Surely that demonstrates Christ's position as somehow lesser than God" is one difficulty commonly raised.

It is true that in His role as bond-servant while on earth, Jesus occupied a lower rank than the Father. Such a rank, however, does not deny His divine nature. In that same passage, Jesus told Philip, "He who has seen Me has seen the Father; how do you say, 'Show us the Father'?" (John 14:8-9). That statement makes clear that Jesus and the Father are one in nature. To have seen one was to have seen the other (compare John 12:44, 45). Therefore, Jesus' words that the Father was greater referred to His temporary *position*, not to His *being*.

Here we will quote extensively from Arthur W. Pink's

excellent work on this passage in his *Exposition of the Gospel of John:*

"My Father is greater than I." This is the favorite verse with Unitarians, who deny the absolute Deity of Christ and His perfect equality with the Father . . . The Savior had just told the apostles that they ought to rejoice because He was going to the Father, and then advances this reason, "*For my Father is greater than I.*" Let this be kept definitely before us and all difficulty vanishes. The Father's being greater than Christ was the reason assigned *why* the disciples should rejoice at their Master's going to the Father. This at once fixes the meaning of the disputed "greater," and shows us the sense in which it was here used. The contrast which the Savior drew between the Father and Himself was *not* concerning *nature,* but official character and position.

Christ was not speaking of Himself in His essential Being. The One who thought it not robbery to be "*equal* with God" had taken the servant form, and not only so, had been made in the likeness of men. In both these senses, namely, in His official status (as Mediator) and in His assumption of human nature, He was inferior to the Father. Throughout this discourse and in the Prayer which follows in chapter 17, the Lord Jesus is represented as the Father's Servant, from whom He had received a commission, and to whom He was to render an account; for whose glory He acted, and under whose authority He spake. But there is another sense, more pertinent, in which the Son was inferior to the Father. In becoming incarnate and tabernacling among men, He had greatly humiliated Himself, by choosing to descend into shame and suffering in their acutest forms. He was now the Son of man that had not where to lay His head. He who was rich had for our sakes become poor. He was the Man of sorrows, and acquainted with grief. In view of this, Christ was now contrasting His *situation* with that of the Father in the heavenly Sanctuary. The Father was seated upon the throne of highest majesty; the brightness of His glory was uneclipsed; He was surrounded by hosts of holy beings, who worshiped Him with uninterrupted praise. Far different was it with His incarnate Son—despised and rejected of men, surrounded by implacable enemies, soon to be nailed to a criminal's cross. In *this* sense, too, He was inferior to the Father. Now in going to the Father, the Son would enjoy a vast improvement of situation. It would be a gain unspeakable. The contrast then was between His present state of humiliation and His coming state of exaltation to the Father! Therefore, those who really loved Him should have rejoiced at the tidings that He *would* go to the Father, because the Father was greater than He, greater both in official status and in surrounding circumstances. It was Christ *owning* His place as Servant, and *magnifying* the One who had sent Him.[1]

God the Father Is the "Head" of Christ

The same relationship of greater and lesser is illustrated in 1 Corinthians 11:3. "But I want you to understand that Christ is the head of every man, and the man is the head of a woman, and God is the head of Christ." In this passage, three comparisons are made: man to Christ, man to woman, and Christ to God. The third comparison between Jesus and God is the one under discussion here. "God is the head of Christ. Doesn't that sound like superiority?" Note that this comparison has to do with patterns of authority; it does not imply inferiority or superiority. Instead, while on earth, in order to identify with humankind, Jesus voluntarily put Himself under the Father's headship.

Jesus Was Subject to the Father

Another verse that shows Christ's relationship to the Father also raises questions. "And when all things are subjected to Him [Jesus], then the Son Himself also will be subjected to the One who subjected all things to Him, that God may be all in all" (1 Corinthians 15:28). Here, the verb *subject* again does not mean *inequality* of persons, but rather a *difference* in roles. Subjection refers only to function, and submission does not necessarily imply inferiority.

Think of it. In order for God to atone for man's sin, someone had to subject Himself to death. Yet only one who had unlimited ability to atone for sin could do that, only a perfect man. He had to have unlimited ability to atone, because He would be shedding His blood for all humankind. He had to be perfect because God accepts only unblemished sacrifices. Who could do that? Only God. And God the Son shed His own blood for us (Acts 20:28). *Obedience* is a key word.

> So then as through one transgression there resulted condemnation to all men, even so through one act of righteousness there resulted justification of life to all men. For as through one man's disobedience the many were made sinners, even so through the obedience of the One the many will be made righteous (Romans 5:18, 19).

As the perfect man, Christ had to be obedient to God and thus fulfill God's plan to redeem humanity. Jesus voluntarily submitted to that plan, to God the Father, in order to save humanity from eternal separation from God.

Jesus Was "Begotten"

Some people maintain that the term "only begotten" in John 3:16 (also 1:14, 18; 3:18) denies Jesus' divinity, implying that He was only another created being. The term "only begotten," however, does not mean created. The word *begotten,* as used in John's Gospel, means "unique, specially blessed, or favored."[2] C. S. Lewis clearly illustrates the meaning of "begotten" when he writes:

> One of the creeds says that Christ is the Son of God "begotten, not created"; and it adds "begotten by his Father before all worlds." Will you please get it quite clear that this has nothing to do with the fact that when Christ was born on earth as a man, that man was the son of a virgin? We are not now thinking about the Virgin Birth. We are thinking about something that happened before Nature was created at all, before time began. "Before all worlds" Christ is begotten, not created. What does it mean?
>
> We don't use the words *begetting* or *begotten* much in modern English, but everyone still knows what they mean. To beget is to become the father of: to create is to make. And the difference is this. When you beget, you beget something of the same kind as yourself. A man begets human babies, a beaver begets little beavers and a bird begets eggs which turn into little birds. But when you make, you make something of a different kind from yourself. A bird makes a nest, a beaver builds a dam, a man makes a wireless set—or he may make something more like himself than a wireless set: say, a statue. If he is a clever enough carver he may make a statue which is very like a man indeed. But, of course, it is not a real man; it only looks like one. It cannot breathe or think. It is not alive.
>
> Now that is the first thing to get clear. What God begets is God; just as what man begets is man. What God creates is not God; just as what man makes is not man. That is why men are not Sons of God in the sense that Christ is. They may be like God in certain ways, but they are not things of the same kind. They are more like statues or pictures of God.
>
> A statue has the shape of a man but it is not alive. In the same way, man has (in a sense I am going to explain) the "shape" or likeness of God, but he has not got the kind of life God has. Let us take the first point (man's resemblance to God) first. Everything God has made has some likeness

to Himself. Space is like Him in its hugeness: not that the greatness of space is the same kind of greatness as God's, but it is a sort of symbol of it, or a translation of it into non-spiritual terms. Matter is like God in having energy: though, again, of course, physical energy is a different kind of thing from the power of God. The vegetable world is like Him because it is alive, and He is the "living God." But life, in this biological sense, is not the same as the life there is in God: it is only a kind of symbol or shadow of it. When we come on to the animals, we find other kinds of resemblance in addition to biological life. The intense activity and fertility of the insects, for example, is a first dim resemblance to the unceasing activity and the creativeness of God. In the higher mammals we get the beginnings of instinctive affection. That is not the same thing as the love that exists in God: but it is like it—rather in the way that a picture drawn on a flat piece of paper can nevertheless be "like" a landscape. When we come to man, the highest of the animals, we get the completest resemblance to God which we know of. (There may be creatures in other worlds who are more like God than man is, but we do not know about them.) Man not only lives, but loves and reasons: biological life reaches its highest known level in him.[3]

In Hebrews 11:17, Isaac is called the "only begotten son" of Abraham, though Abraham had two sons, Isaac and Ishmael. Thus the writer of Hebrews was using "begotten" in its "unique, specially blessed, or favored" sense. The same is true in John 3:16 of Jesus (the only difference being that God had one Son and Abraham had two).

Monogenes, the word translated "only begotten," is formed from two words. *Monos* means "single, only, sole, lone." *Genes* means "offspring, progeny, race, kind, sort, species." It is a compound word; it means a unique kind.

Jesus Was a Man

A possible stumbling block that might keep some individuals from accepting the divinity of Christ is that Jesus is clearly said in the Bible to have been a man. For example, one reads, "For there is one God, and one mediator also between God and men, the man Christ Jesus" (1 Timothy 2:5). Romans 5:12-21 speaks of sin being atoned for through the "Man, Jesus Christ" (v.15).

Although it is true that Scripture teaches that Jesus was human, it also teaches that He was divine. He was a man, born of the Virgin Mary, but He was also God (John 1:1, 14; 20:28; Colossians 2:9; Titus 2:13; 2 Peter 1:1, Hebrews 1:8). Paul emphasized Jesus' divinity, saying his message came not from men nor from a "man" but from "Jesus Christ" (Galatians 1:1). Jesus was a "man," but also "Yahweh," "Son of God," "Lord of lords," "King of kings" and "the Alpha and the Omega."

Jesus Was Called the First-Born of Creation

Some people get confused over the word *first-born,* thinking it must mean "first-created." That would imply that Jesus was only a created being, not preexistent, or eternal, or God.

"First-born," however, does not mean "first-created." When Paul stated that Christ was "the first-born of all creation" (Colossians 1:15), he used the Greek word *prototokos* which meant "heir, first in rank." Had he intended to say *first-created,* he would have used the Greek word for first-created, *protoktistos.* Nowhere in Scripture does it say that God "created" Jesus.

In his *Theology on the Person of Christ* Lewis Sperry Chafer states: "This title—sometimes translated *First-Born*—indicates that Christ is First-Born, the elder in relation to all creation; not the first created thing, but the antecedent to all things as well as the cause of them (Colossians 1:16)."[4] Jesus could not have been the first created being and also the agent by which all creation came to be as is claimed for Him in Scripture. If he was the agent of *all* creation then He, Himself could not be created.

Jesus and God Were "One in Agreement"

Jesus said, ". . . I give eternal life to them, and they shall never perish; and no one shall snatch them out of My hand. My Father, who has given them to Me, is greater than all; and no one is able to snatch them out of the Father's hand. I and the Father are one" (John 10:28-30). Was Jesus claiming to be one and the same as God (i.e., as ice and water are "one" in nature); or was He claiming only to have a oneness, unity of purpose, or agreement with God? The text indicates the former.

First, the Jews to whom He was speaking—who culturally were in a position to interpret His words better than anyone 2,000 years later—understood Jesus to be saying He was "God." They took up stones to stone him ". . . for blasphemy. . . because You, being a man, make Yourself out to be God" (John 10:33). Second, in Greek, the word *one* is neuter (*hen*), not masculine (*heis*), which indicates that Jesus and God were one and the same in essence. The masculine form would mean they were one person, which would deny the *personal* distinction between the Father and the Son.

The section of John that follows is Jesus' response to the charge of blasphemy. To a Jew versed in the Law, His words made sense. To anyone unacquainted with the Jewish understanding of the Old Testament, it can be a difficult and easily misunderstood passage, especially as it relates to the matter of the deity of Christ. The passage reads:

> Jesus answered them, "Has it not been written in your Law, 'I said, you are gods'? If he called them gods, to whom the word of God came (and the Scripture cannot be broken), do you say of Him, whom the Father sanctified and sent into the world, 'You are blaspheming,' because I said, 'I am the Son of God'? If I do not do the works of My Father, do not believe Me; but if I do them, though you do not believe Me, believe the works, that you may know and understand that the Father is in Me, and I in the Father." Therefore they were seeking again to seize Him; and He eluded their grasp (John 10:34-39).

Much of the confusion has to do with Jesus' use of the word *gods* (v.34). Was He saying: "Other men have been called 'gods.' Why cannot I call myself the 'Son of God'?" (thereby indirectly calling Himself a man, not divine)?

The phrase, "I said, you are gods," is found in Psalm 82:6. The word *gods* used in the Psalm is the Hebrew word *elohim* (*eloah* = "god," *im* = plural ending = "gods"). The fact that God is often referred to as *Elohim* in the Old Testament does not mean that the Bible teaches a form of polytheism (many gods). Throughout the Old Testament the *singular form of the verb* is always used with *Elohim* when speaking of God ("In the beginning God [plural: *Elohim*] created [singular] the heavens and the earth"—Genesis 1:1). If anything, the language of the Bible is consistent with the doctrine of the Trinity, just as in Matthew 28:19 the noun *name* (singular in Greek) is used to express "the Father, the Son, and the Holy Spirit." They comprise one "name." The term "gods" (*elohim*) in Psalm 82 refers to Jewish "judges," men who were to act as "God" (or "gods") on behalf of the people, "god" in the sense of being just, fair, etc. Obviously, they were not literally "God." Exodus 21:1-6 and 22:9, 28 use the same term; the word translated "judges" in our English Bibles actually is *elohim*.

That was the Old Testament context to which Jesus was referring. Why? Seemingly, Jesus was asking them why they were so upset by the use of the term "Son of God." They had been exposed to it before (i.e., men being called "gods" in Psalm 82). The issue before them was this: "Don't stop at the use of the term. Look at Me. Look at My works. Are they from God? If they are, believe what I say, including the names I give Myself."

Obviously, Jesus was not denying His earlier claim of deity. He was making a bold statement, challenging the Jews to decide if His works gave credence to His claims ("I and the Father are one").

The argument is from a lesser to a greater. If God called men "gods" figuratively, how much more appropriate it is for the one whom "the Father sanctified and sent into the world" (that was certainly not true of the Old Testament judges) to call Himself the Son of God. He was in fact doing the works of the Father: raising the dead, imparting eternal life, sustaining creation, altering creation (changing water to wine, calming storms, etc.).

Jesus Had Limited Knowledge

As a human being, Jesus had limited knowledge. Speaking of His second coming, He said, "But of that day or hour no one knows, not even the angels in heaven, nor the Son, but the Father alone" (Mark 13:32). As discussed earlier, Jesus in his role as "bond-servant" chose to live life on human terms while on earth, trusting in His Father's power, not His own. For example, He said, ". . . the Son can do nothing of Himself" (John 5:19). "I can do nothing on My own initiative" (John 5:30). "I always do the things that are pleasing to Him" (John 8:29). "The Father abiding in Me does His works" (John 14:10).

Thus, when Jesus, in the form of a man, said that He did not know the hour of His return, it could have been because of His self-imposed limitations as a bond-servant. Not that He was not equal to God, but rather in this instance that He had chosen not to exercise all His divine prerogatives.

"No One Except God Is Good"

A man once approached Jesus and said, "Good Teacher. . ." Jesus interrupted Him: "Why do you call Me good? No one is good except God alone" (Mark 10:17-18). At first glance it may seem that Jesus was denying His divinity. He was not. Rather, He was underscoring that God alone was good. Scripture is clear. Jesus was "sinless," "holy," "innocent," "righteous," "separate from sinners," and "undefiled" (Acts 3:14; 2 Corinthians 5:21; Hebrews 4:15; 7:26: 1 Peter 2:22; 1 John 3:5). By all standards of goodness, Jesus was truly "good." Thus, Jesus shared an attribute of God: goodness.

A possible reason for Jesus' response to the man's statement was to gauge the depth of his awareness of who He was, and how serious his intent was to follow Him. As soon as Jesus told the man that there is none good but God, He asked the man to sell His possessions and follow Him as a disciple. Note that He did not say "Follow God," but

"Follow Me." Contrary to first impressions, this passage lends strong support to Christ's deity.

In conclusion, almost all of the arguments used to deny that Jesus is God stem from a misunderstanding of Philippians 2:6-11, which teaches that Jesus had two natures, the human and the divine. Jesus "existed" in two "forms," as God (v.6) and as a man ("bond-servant," v. 7). The text teaches that His first state was a position of "equality" with God, the second a "humbled" state. Almost all of the verses used to argue that Jesus was unequal to God the Father, and therefore not one with God, compare Jesus in His humble state as a man with God's exalted position in heaven. The fact is overlooked that Jesus left His exalted position of equality with God the Father in order to become a man, die for the sins of the world, be resurrected, and then once again be exalted.

Chapter 8

Is Jesus Christ Your Lord?

At some point, after examining the evidence, one must decide whether one is going to believe in the deity of Christ or not. That Jesus lived, died, was buried, and rose again, most persons who call themselves Christians would agree. Yet Jesus said, ". . . Unless you believe that *I am [ego eimi]*, you shall die in your sins" (John 8:24). Paul wrote, ". . . if you confess with your mouth *Jesus* as Lord, and believe in your heart that God raised Him from the dead, you shall be saved" (Romans 10:9). If Christ is divine, and if belief in His divinity is necessary for salvation, much is at stake.

C. S. Lewis brought the point of Christ's divinity to the fore when he wrote a letter to a skeptical friend, Arthur Greeves:

> I think the great difficulty is this: If He was *not* God, who or what was He? In Matthew 28:19 you already get the baptismal formula "In the name of the Father, the Son & the Holy Ghost." Who is this "Son"? Is the Holy Ghost a man? If not, does a man "send" Him (see John 15:26)? In Col. 1:12 Christ is "before all things and by Him all things consist." What sort of a man is this? I leave out the obvious place at the beginning of St. John's Gospel. Take something much less obvious. When He weeps over Jerusalem (Matthew 23) why does He suddenly say (v.34) "*I* send unto you prophets and wise men"? *Who* could say this except either God or a lunatic? Who is this man who goes about forgiving sins? Or what about Mark 2:18-19. What man can

announce that simply because he is present, acts of penitence, such as fasting, are "off"? Who can give the school a half holiday except the Headmaster?

The doctrine of Christ's divinity seems to me not something stuck on which you can unstick but something that peeps out at every point so that you would have to unravel the whole web to get rid of it. Of course you may reject some of these passages as unauthentic, but then I could do the same to yours if I cared to play that game! When it says God cannot be tempted I take this to be an obvious truth. God, as God, cannot, any more than He can die. He became man precisely to do and suffer what as God He could not do and suffer. And if you take away the godhead of Christ, what is Christianity all *about*? How can the death of one man have this effect for all men which is proclaimed throughout the New Testament?[1]

This is exactly the point—no one man could have any special effect on all humanity. Only God the Son could atone for all humankind. No partial substitute would satisfy.

Our redemption, the crucial point on which all of Christianity rests, is dependent on Jesus Christ's being not only man but also God. Our "passover lamb"—Jesus Christ tortured, crucified, dead, and buried—had to be a sheep from the flock. God would hardly qualify as one of our brethren, yet His Son could.

Many who deny the deity of Christ maintain that things like the Trinity or the two natures of Christ are "impossible" or "unreasonable." They would say, "God could never have been nailed to a cross; God is Spirit" or "God would not offer Himself to Himself" or "God cannot be born." Those statements ignore the fact of the incarnation, that it was the Son who offered Himself to the Father, that with God all things are possible.

We should not let our concepts of "reasonable" or "possible" sit in judgment on what God has revealed. The issue is what God has said, not can we fully comprehend it?

In reading the Gospel narratives, we see that Jesus evoked three primary responses from the people of His day: hatred, terror, or adoration. Having understood His claims, people were unable to remain neutral. Jesus set the stage for every individual either to accept Him or to reject Him.

Peter, who denied Jesus three times, eventually died a martyr's death because of His conviction that Jesus was the Christ in human flesh. When Christ asked Peter who He was, Peter confessed: "Thou art the Christ, the Son of the living God" (Matthew 16:16). Jesus responded to Peter's confession, not by correcting his conclusion, but by acknowledging its validity and source: "Blessed are you, Simon Barjona, because flesh and blood did not reveal this to you, but My Father who is in heaven" (Matthew 16:17).

Thomas was often referred to as the doubter, because he questioned Christ's resurrection. Finally, after overwhelming evidence by Christ Himself after the resurrection, Thomas cried out in acknowledgement and worship: "My Lord and my God!" (John 20:28).

Since then, many people through the centuries have experienced a similar struggle when confronted with Jesus' question, "Who do you say that I am?" We are faced with a trilemma that is depicted in the diagram on the following page.

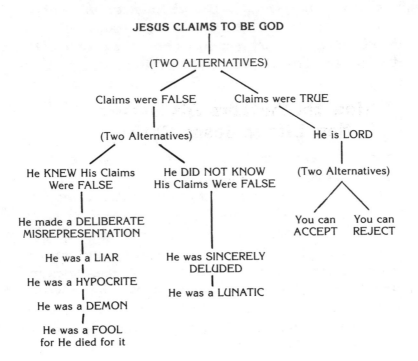

For further explanation of the above diagram, see *Evidence That Demands A Verdict*[1] (chapter 7) and *More Than a Carpenter*[2] (chapter 2). For further historical evidence supporting the deity of Christ, read *The Resurrection Factor*.[3]

What about you? What do you think of Christ? Do you have a mere religion, or do you have a personal relationship with the living God through His Son Jesus Christ? There is ample evidence to support one's belief in the deity of Christ for those willing to make a decision. After Thomas cried out to Jesus, "My Lord and my God!" Jesus replied, "Because you have seen Me, have you believed? Blessed are they who did not see, and yet believed" (John 20:29).

Chapter 9

How the Authors Discovered
New Life in Jesus Christ

Bart

"My own questioning about the significance of Christianity—more than just the Sunday school routine—began as a kid watching Billy Graham on television. Until then I'd written most Christians off as either hypocrites or eccentrics, neither of which seemed particularly appealing. As I listened to Dr. Graham preach, I felt as if my heart was going to explode. Though subjective, I felt God's presence in the room with me.

One thought Dr. Graham conveyed was that God was absolutely pure and blameless and that we were sinful (i.e., we've all actively and passively rebelled against God and missed His mark of perfection). It was like the guy who said, "But judge, look at all the people I didn't kill!" The point was that we all stand guilty before a holy and righteous God, and would only pollute and corrupt heaven if we went there without having a basic change in nature.

As much as I wanted to deny it, I felt the guilt. I hadn't lived up to my own standards, let alone God's. Dr. Graham said that going to church wasn't enough. It didn't make you a Christian (any more than going to a garage makes you a car), and that becoming a Christian involved an active, not a passive believing.

It's like the man who tightrope-walked Niagara Falls with a 200-pound sack of sand on his back. After crossing, he asked a spectator, "Do you believe I could do it again?" The person said, "Sure!" So the guy tossed down the sack and said, "Climb on my back."

Real believing is more than just giving mental assent to the claims of Christianity. It is being willing to "climb on" and lay our lives on the line. Anything short of that is not "believing" in the biblical sense of the word.

I once heard a story about a judge whose own daughter was brought into his court on speeding charges. To everyone's surprise, he gave her the stiffest fine possible. Then he stepped down off his bench, pulled out his wallet, and paid the fine for her. Thus, both the law's demands for justice and the love of a father's heart were fully satisfied. Dr. Graham spoke of how God had done this in the person of Jesus—God stepping down to become a man and die for humankind because he loved us.

Dr. Graham went on to say that we had to be willing to admit our sin and receive God's forgiveness through faith in Christ's death and resurrection for us. We could never earn it or pay for it. It was a gift we could either accept or reject.

Well, I put off becoming a Christian for several years, partly because it took me awhile before I met some Christians I respected and partially because I was still confused as to what I had to *do* to become a Christian. But finally the day came. A speaker told me *how* to become a Christian in a non-threatening environment. (I had turned down other opportunities where I ran the risk of being embarrassed. I was afraid that it wouldn't work and that I'd just make a fool of myself.)

So, as I sat in my seat at a high school rally in Topeka, Kansas, I quietly prayed and asked Christ to come into my life. To my great surprise He did! I found a peace I had never known before. Old feelings of guilt were gone, and I had a new joy and a reason for living. I was happily surprised to see God actually answer prayer. He cared!

Even as a Christian I sometimes used to feel like an abandoned baby that was put in a basket and dropped on God's doorstep, and that God, being the loving God He is, had no choice but to take me in. Now I know that is not so, for out of His great love He *chose* me (Ephesians 1:4, 5). To all who will come, He says, "Come!"

As someone who cares and has come to know His love, I can only encourage you, the reader, not to remain neutral. He loves you and proved it by becoming a man and dying for you. This is what the incarnation and deity of Christ is all about, and why Josh and I have written this book.

Josh[1]

I set out intellectually to refute the Bible as a reliable historical document and the resurrection as a factual historical event and Christianity as a relevant alternative. After gathering the evidence, some of which has been shared in my books, I was compelled to conclude that my arguments wouldn't stand up, that Jesus Christ was exactly who He claimed to be—the Son of God.

The above conclusion about the historical reliability of the Bible and the person of Christ brought with it an intense struggle. My mind was telling me that all this was true, but my will was pulling me in another direction. I discovered that to become a Christian can be an earth shaking experience.

Guilt was evident in my life. Jesus Christ made a direct challenge to my will to trust Him as Savior, as the one who died on the cross for my sins. Let me paraphrase His invitation: "Look! I have been standing at the door and I am constantly knocking. If anyone hears Me calling him and opens the door, I will come in" (Revelation 3:20).

"But as many as received Him, to them He gave the right to become children of God, even to those who believe in His name" (John 1:12). I didn't care if He did walk on water, or turn water into wine. I didn't want a party pooper invading my life. I couldn't think of a faster way to ruin a good time, or to destroy intellectual pursuit and impede scholarly acceptability with my peers.

So there I was: My mind told me on the one hand that Christianity was true and my will said, "Don't admit it." Every time I was around those enthusiastic Christians, the conflict would intensify. If you've ever been around happy people when you're miserable, you understand how they can bug you. They would be so happy and I would feel so miserable I would literally get up and run right out of the room.

It came to the point where I'd go to bed at ten at night and I wouldn't fall asleep until four in the morning. I knew I had to get Jesus off my mind or go out of my mind!

New Life Begins

Being open-minded and intellectually convinced, on December 19, 1959, at 8:30 p.m. during my second year at the university, I became a Christian.

Someone asked me, "How do you know?"

I said, "Look, I was there."

That night I prayed. I prayed four things in order to establish a relationship with God—a personal relationship with His Son, the resurrected, living Christ. Over a period of time that relationship has transformed my life.

First, I prayed, "Lord Jesus, thank You for dying on the

cross for me." Second, I said, "I confess those things in my life that aren't pleasing to You and ask You to forgive me and cleanse me." (The Bible says, "Though your sins are as scarlet, they will be as white as snow.") Third, I said, "Right now, in the best way I know how, I open the door of my heart and life and trust You as my Savior and Lord. Take control of my life. Change me from the inside out. Make me the type of person You created me to be."

The last thing I prayed was, "Thank You for coming into my life by faith." It was a faith produced by the Holy Spirit, based on evidence and on the facts of history and on God's Word.

I'm sure you've heard religious people talk about their "bolt of lightning." Well, after I prayed, nothing happened. I mean nothing. In fact, after I made that decision, I felt worse. I felt I was going to vomit. I felt sick deep down.

"Oh no, McDowell, what'd you get sucked into now?" I wondered. I really felt I'd gone off the deep end—and some of my friends agreed.

Changes

But I can tell you one thing: In six months to a year and a half, I found I hadn't gone off the deep end. My life was changed.

I was in a debate with the head of the history department at a midwestern university, and I said "My life has been changed." He interrupted me rather sarcastically. "McDowell, are you trying to tell us that God really changed your life in the 20th century? What areas?"

After 45 minutes of my describing changes, he said, "Okay, that's enough."

Mental Peace. One area I told him about was my restless-ness. I was a person who always had to be occupied. I had to be over at my girl's place or somewhere in a rap session. I'd walk across campus, and my mind would be a whirlwind of conflicts. I'd sit down and try to study or think, and I couldn't.

But a few months after I made that decision to trust Christ, a kind of mental peace began to develop. Don't misunderstand. I'm not talking about the absence of con-flict. What I found in this relationship with Jesus wasn't so much the absence of conflict as it was the ability to cope with it. I wouldn't trade this for anything in the world.

Control of Temper. Another area that started to change was my bad temper. I used to "blow my stack" if somebody just looked at me cross-eyed. I still have the scars from almost killing a man my first year in the university. My temper was such an integral part of me that I didn't con-sciously seek to change it.

One day after my decision to put my faith in Christ, I arrived at a crisis, only to find that my temper was gone! And only once in the past twenty-four years have I lost it.

A Man I Hated

There's another area I'm not proud of. I mention it because a lot of people need to have the same change in their lives through a relationship with the resurrected, living Christ. This is the area of hatred (one might say bitterness).

I had a lot of hatred in my life. It wasn't something out-wardly manifested, but there was a kind of inward grinding. I was ticked off with people, things, issues. Like so many other people, I was insecure. Every time I met someone different from me, he became a threat.

The one person I hated more than anyone else in the

world was my father. I despised him. He was the town alcoholic. If you're from a small town and one of your parents is an alcoholic, you know what I'm talking about.

Everybody knew. My friends would come to high school and make jokes about my father being downtown. They didn't think it bothered me. I was laughing on the outside, but let me tell you I was crying on the inside. I'd go out in the barn and see my mother lying in the manure behind the cows. She'd been knocked down by my father and couldn't get up.

When we had friends over, I would take my father, tie him up in the barn, and park the car up around the silo. We would tell our friends he had to go somewhere so we wouldn't be embarrassed. I don't think any person could hate another person more than I hated my father.

Hatred Becomes Love

Maybe five months after I made that decision for Christ, love for my father—a love from God through Jesus Christ—inundated my life. That love took my hatred and turned it upside down. That love was so strong, I was able to look my father squarely in the eyes and say, "Dad, I love you." I really meant it. After some of the things I'd done, that shook him up.

Shortly after I transferred to a private university, I was in a serious car accident. With my neck in traction, I was taken home. I'll never forget my father coming into my room and asking, "Son, how can you love a father like me?" I said, "Dad, six months ago I despised you." Then I shared with him my conclusions about Jesus Christ.

"Dad, I let Christ come into my life," I said. "I can't explain it completely. But as a result of this relationship, I've found the capacity to love and accept not only you, but other people just the way they are."

Forty-five minutes later one of the greatest thrills of my life occurred. Somebody in my own family, someone who knew me so well I couldn't pull the wool over his eyes—my own father—said to me, "Son, if God can do in my life what I've seen Him do in yours, then I want to give Him the opportunity." Right there my father prayed with me and trusted Christ.

Usually changes take place over several days, weeks, or months . . . even years. The life of my father was changed right before my eyes. It was as though somebody reached in and turned on a light bulb. I've never seen such a rapid change before or since. My father touched alcohol only once after that. He got it as far as his lips and that was it. He didn't need it any more.

It Works

I've come to one conclusion. A relationship with Jesus Christ changes lives. You can ignorantly laugh at Christianity; you can mock and ridicule it. But it works. It changes lives. If you trust Christ, start watching your attitudes and actions—because Jesus Christ is in the business of changing lives, forgiving sin and removing guilt.

It's Your Choice

Christianity is not something that can be forced on someone or shoved down someone's throat. You have your life to live, and I have mine. All I can do is tell you what I've learned. Beyond that, it's your decision. My wife puts it this way: "Because Christ was raised from the dead, He lives. And because He lives, He has that infinite capacity to enter a man or woman's life, forgive them, and change them from the inside out."

The key element is the resurrection factor. Christ is risen.

It's Personal

I've shared how I personally responded to the claims of Christ. You also need to ask the logical question: "What difference does all this evidence make to me? What difference does it make whether or not I believe Christ rose again and died on the cross for my sins?" The answer is put best by something Jesus said to a man who doubted, Thomas. He told him: "I am the way, and the truth, and the life; no one comes to the Father, but through Me" (John 14:6).

On the basis of all the evidence for Christ's resurrection, and considering the fact that Jesus offers forgiveness of sin and an eternal relationship with God, who would be so foolhardy as to reject Him? Christ is alive. He is living today.

You can trust God right now by faith through prayer. Prayer is talking with God. God knows your heart and is not so concerned with your words as He is with the attitude of your heart. If you have never trusted Christ, you can do so right now.

The prayer I prayed is: "Lord Jesus, I need You. Thank You for dying on the cross for my sins. I open the door of my life and trust You as my Savior. Thank You for forgiving my sins and giving me eternal life. Make me the kind of person You want me to be. Thank You that I can trust You."

An Offer to You

If you have trusted Christ, or believe you are going to do so in the near future, write me. You will have a lot of questions, as I had after my decision. A professor once shared with me some principles that made sense to me about how my life could be changed through this new relationship with God through Christ. I have put these principles into letter form and would like to send them to you.

Josh McDowell
P.O. Box 5585
Richardson, TX 75080

Appendix

Various Views About the Deity of Christ

We felt it would be helpful to list a number of religious systems and summarize, as best we could, their views on the deity of Christ. For those interested in a more comprehensive discussion, see the *Handbook of Today's Religions* series by Josh McDowell and Don Stewart, available at your Christian bookstore or from Here's Life Publishers, Inc., San Bernardino, California.

Agnostic
The word *agnostic* comes from two Greek words, *a* meaning "no," and *gnosis* meaning "knowledge." Simply put, an agnostic is one who claims it is not possible to know whether there is a God or not, let alone whether Christ is God.

Atheist
The word *atheist* comes from two Greek words, *a* meaning "no," and *theos* meaning "God." An atheist believes that there is no God.

Bahai
The Bahai faith teaches that in the history of the world many religions have led to God. God has used many prophets as His divine spokesmen, Jesus being the main one for His day, as were Buddha, Moses, Krishna, Zoroaster, Muhammad, etc., for theirs. Bahais believe that Baha'u'llah

is God's prophet for today.

Black Muslims
The Black Muslims are an American Islamic movement, with strong political and racial overtones. Like many movements, it has tended to mellow with the passing of time. Certain segments of Christianity are integrated into this movement with Christ sometimes being spoken of as black. Jesus is considered a prophet of Allah (God), inferior to Muhammad as a prophet, and was definitely not God.

Buddhism
Buddhism, which began as a philosophy espoused by Siddhartha Gautama (Buddha), became a religion approximately two hundred years after his death when a segment of his followers deified him. Buddha (the name means "enlightened one") is treated as a savior-god, even though he claimed to be only a teacher. Buddhists view Jesus as a moral teacher of less importance than Buddha—prayer is offered to Buddha. The main God of Buddhism is impersonal.

Children of God (Family Of Love)
This group was founded by David Brandt Berg, nicknamed Mo (for Moses) by his followers and considered a prophet. It is not clear in his writings whether or not he believes the deity of Christ.

Christian Science
Founded by Mary Baker Eddy, this group denies the deity of Christ, asserting that Jesus is the son of God, not God. Christian Science teaches that "Jesus" is the human man and "Christ" the divine idea that heals.

Confucianism
Confucianism, named for Confucius, is a Chinese philosophy and political system more than a religion (although it promotes worship of mountains, rivers, ancestors, etc.). In its system, "heaven" is the highest spiritual reality and is used in place of the name "God." Confucianism is humanistic in its concerns, stressing love, peace, and gentleness in all levels of society. It tends to pay little attention to the supernatural, and rejects the Judeo-Christian concept of a personal God.

Divine Light Mission
This movement, founded by Guru Maharaj Ji, is Hindu in origin. It teaches that God has revealed his knowledge through several divine Masters in the past (Jesus, Krishna, etc.). Maharaj Ji is seen as the new Master to lead men and women today to a knowledge of the truth.

Eckankar
Eckankar, allegedly the science of soul-travel, was founded by Paul Twitchell, a "prophet, healer, soul-traveler." It is a blend of Western Christianity and Eastern religions. Like the Bahai faith, it gives each of the main religions credence in helping one know God. Eckankar speaks of a Holy Spirit through whom we come to know "Divine Reality" and enter into a "God-realized" state. Jesus is treated as a man who had a "Christ-consciousness." As in Hinduism, Sugmad, the "Supreme Being," is thought to have incarnated himself in many masters or gurus (such as Jesus).

EST (Erhard Seminars Training)
EST was started by John Paul Rosenberg, who now goes by the name of Werner Erhard. Its high-priced seminars are programmed to change one's thinking about reality. EST is a philosophy of no absolutes. Whatever "IS" (est) is right

(whether good, bad, evil, etc.); there is no such thing as wrong (except perhaps in your mind). Each person is his or her own god.

Hare Krishna (*ISKCON*—International Society for Krishna Consciousness)

The Hare Krishna movement is rooted in Hinduism. Its Bible, the Bhagavad-Gita, is supposedly the summation of India's Vedic Literature (sacred writings). Krishna is the "Supreme Personality of Godhead," the one full of knowledge, and cause of all causes. As in Hinduism, ISKCON believes in many gods. Brahma, the impersonal world soul (the closest equivalent to "God"), has manifested himself in millions of gods, the highest being Krishna. Krishna is called "Lord" and receives prayer. He has supposedly appeared as a man at various times (Buddha was supposedly one of his incarnations). The Christian concepts of God and Christ are rejected.

Hinduism

Hinduism grew out of India's nomadic oral tradition and sacred writings (called Vedas). It has no single founder. Brahma is seen as the all-encompassing world soul behind the universe, impersonal, but manifested in millions of gods, many of which are in nature. Hinduism is pantheistic, seeing all things (trees, etc.) as part of Brahma. Jesus is seen as a special manifestation of Brahma, just slightly more so than any other person. All people are considered spirits (*atman*) that somehow got separated from Brahma. The main goal of life, according to Hinduism, is to be absorbed back into Brahma.

I-Ching

I-Ching (the *I* is pronounced *E*) means Book of Changes. It is a very complex method of seeking spiritual guidance through the use of the I-Ching book. It is Chinese in origin and existed prior to the time of Christ. It had a major influence on Confucianism and Taoism and is once again becoming popular with many Eastern religions and sects, as well as among young people with no particular religious ties.

Islam
Islam is a religion believing in one God, Allah. Its adherents are called Muslims. Jesus is viewed as a prophet, along with Adam, Noah, Abraham, Moses, etc. Most of the New Testament accounts of the life of Jesus are rejected by Muslims as false and historically inaccurate (e.g., they believe that Judas died on the cross, not Jesus). Muhammad, the founder of Islam, is considered Allah's chief prophet.

Jainism
Jainism, founded by Mahavira, is an Eastern religion that grew out of Hinduism. It does not believe in a supreme being. Mahavira is considered a savior by Jainists, who adhere to an ascetic, nonviolent lifestyle, trying to rid themselves of negative karma (bad deeds that stick to the soul). Jainists try to deny themselves of all pleasure and anything that would bind their allegiance to this world.

Jehovah's Witnesses
The Jehovah's Witnesses movement, founded by Charles Taze Russell, teaches that Christ was a pre-existent "god" who was created by God—through whom God then created the world. That is, Christ is considered to have been a sinless spirit being (a god), who was made flesh. The Jehovah's Witnesses' view of the deity of Christ comes close to that of Arius, who denied the deity of Christ at the Council of Nicea. Nor is the Holy Spirit considered God—only Jehovah.

Judaism

Judaism has taken many turns through the centuries. One can be a Jew either by nationality or by religion. For example, one can be an atheist or an agnostic and still be a Jew by birth. Or one can be born a Gentile, convert to Judaism religiously and thus, in one sense of the word, be Jewish. The early Christian church was entirely Jewish. Judaism and Christianity were not and need not be mutually exclusive. There are many messianic Jews (or Hebrew Christians) who are followers of Christ, who see Him as their Messiah and Lord. By and large, however, Jews through the centuries have rejected Jesus as their Messiah. Many still believe in the God of Abraham, although only a relatively small percentage accept all of the Old Testament as literally true. Some Jews say that Jesus was well intentioned or a good teacher. Many, however, see Him as either deluded or a fraud.

Mormonism

The Mormon church was founded by Joseph Smith. Shortly after his death there was a split over who was to be his successor. The main body of followers, who became known as Mormons, acknowledged Brigham Young as their new leader. Mormons believe in many "Gods." They teach that a council of the Gods met, and that one of them, Adam (as in Genesis chapter two), became a man and is the "God" of this planet. He is the one Jesus referred to as "God the Father" (see *Journal of Discourses,* Vol. I, pp. 50, 51). Mormons believe that all people exist first in a pre-mortal state, and that in order to become Gods we must first take upon ourselves bodies of flesh and bone. They teach that Jesus as a pre-mortal man was the brother of Lucifer, and that Jesus had several wives. *Elohim and Jehovah* (two Old Testament names for God) are seen as two separate Gods.

New Age Movement

The New Age Movement is a loose term for many religious, political, and social organizations, along with many people who consider themselves "New Age" but have no allegiance to any group. Many, if not most, within the movement are probably unaware of any one underlying philosophy. However, an organized segment of the New Age Movement ran full-page ads in major newspapers and magazines around the world in April, 1982, announcing that the Christ was on earth and soon to be revealed. That segment believes that the World Soul (Buddhist concept) has incarnated himself four times in the history of the world and that incarnation number five (Lord Maitreya) is on earth waiting for the proper time to reveal himself.

Radio Church of God

This church, founded by Herbert W. Armstrong, has been carried on by his son, Garner Ted Armstrong. The Armstrongs believe in the deity of Christ, but not in the orthodox sense of the word. For them, the whole "family" of believers will eventually comprise the very being of God ("We shall then be God!"). They do not believe in the Trinity.

Reorganized Church of Later Day Saints

This church and the Mormons both have Joseph Smith as their founder, and both churches adhere to the Book of Mormon (Mormons accept several other books as well). After Joseph Smith's death, the church split, with the Mormon branch following Brigham Young and the Reorganized Church of LDS following Joseph Smith's son. The latter is much more orthodox in its views. They believe in the deity of Christ and Trinity, even though there is evidence that Joseph Smith did not. (Two months prior to his assassination, Joseph Smith said in a speech that the Father had been a man just as Jesus had been a man—a view consistent with present-day Mormonism).

Scientology (Church of Scientology)

Scientology, self-designated as the "science of knowing how to know" or "applied religious philosophy," is rooted in the world of science fiction rather than in the Judeo-Christian tradition. It does not discuss doctrines like the Trinity and the deity of Christ. Its founder, fantasy writer L. Ron Hubbard, published a book called *Dianetics: the Modern Science* (1950) introducing his theories and therapeutic techniques. Scientology, which now sells its services, has an unusual, specialized vocabulary for its concepts and procedures.

Shintoism

Shintoism is a Japanese religion that believes in many gods. It is politically tied to the Japanese way of life and is very accommodating to Buddhist beliefs (i.e., Buddhist priests often perform ceremonial rites for Shintos). Shintoism has no one set of religious beliefs, but is divided into many sects.

Sikhism

Sikhism, founded by Nanak in the late 1400s, is a branch of Hinduism. God is considered formless, sovereign, unknowable, and absolute. Unlike Hinduism, the religion is basically monotheistic, and does not have all the ritualism that Hinduism has. Like Hinduism, however, the final goal in life is to be absorbed into God.

Spiritism

Spiritism is a broad classification that encompasses many spiritual practices and beliefs (seances, soothsayers, mediums, magic, sorcery, palm readers, astrologers, horoscopes, etc.). Such practices and beliefs have been around for thousands of years. Depending on the person involved in spiritism, most (although not all) reject the deity of Christ. Of special importance is the Bible's teaching that such people are opening themselves up to demonic spirits by seeking spiritual guidance from someone or something other than God—practices condemned in Scripture.

Theosophy
Theosophy, a movement started by Helena Blavatsky, teaches that the underlying cause of all religions is the same; an impersonal God or Divine Principle. The ultimate end of all religions, whichever one chooses, is to be absorbed into God. For Blavatsky, Christ was the Divine Principle, Jesus the man.

Transcendental Meditation (TM)
TM was founded by Maharishi Mahesh Yogi and thus its origins are Hindu. Superficially, TM seems to be more of a philosophy than a religion, with emphasis on inner peace, relaxation, meditation, and psychological wholeness. The religious teachings and ceremonies of TM, however, are strongly Hinduwith Western applications. Christ is viewed as a good moral teacher.

Unification Church
The Unification Church (or the Moonies, as the group is called) was founded by Sun Myung Moon of Korea. Jesus is said to be the son of God, not God. Unification teaches that Jesus brought spiritual redemption to earth but died prematurely. Sun Myung Moon is seen as the new Messiah to bring physical redemption to earth and finish what Jesus failed to complete. The Holy Spirit is seen as the feminine counterpart to God the Father.

Unitarianism
Unitarianism, while considered a religion, puts humanity and humanitarian concerns, not God, at the center. The church has no formulated creed concerning God, Jesus,

salvation, the Bible, or any other theological doctrines. It stresses total freedom of religious belief. God is generally thought to be impersonal.

Unity

The Unity School of Christianity, started by Mr. and Mrs. Charles Fillmore, is close to Christian Science. God, considered impersonal, is "Life" or the "Divine Principle." Sin is defined as negative thinking, Jesus is man, and Christ the divine idea. The Bible is treated allegorically. By means of Unity's Metaphysical Dictionary, the Bible can be interpreted to gain truth and proper thinking.

The Way International

The Way International, founded by Dr. Victor Paul Wierwille, teaches that Jesus was a sinless man, the Messiah, our redeemer, the Son of God, but not God. Adherents deny the pre-existence and eternalness of Christ; Jesus's existence began at conception in the womb of Mary. Unlike most other groups that deny the Trinity and deity of Christ, Way members claim to hold a literal interpretation of the Bible. (As such, they should be very open to examining its contents.) The Way teaches that God is holy and God is Spirit, but when Scripture speaks of the Holy Spirit (spelled holy spirit), it is referring to a spiritual gift that God gives.

Zen Buddhism

Zen Buddhism is the name given to a segment of Buddhism that emphasizes meditation to discover one's Buddha-nature and reality. Zen is a blend of Buddhism and Taoism. As in Buddhism, deity is identified with nature. God is an unconscious, impersonal essence found in all things; members thus have a keen awareness of art and other aesthetic expressions. Jesus is looked on as a good moral teacher.

Zoroastrianism

Zoroastrianism grew out of the same Vedic traditions and sacred writings as did Hinduism. Zoroaster, the founder, emphasized worship of only one god, Ahura Mazda ("Wise Lord"); his outlook was thus basically monotheistic. Zoroastrianism believes in a holy spirit and an evil spirit, a duality vying for human souls.

Notes

Chapter 1

1. For the reader who has difficulty accepting these facts without further documentation, we suggest a study of *Evidence That Demands A Verdict,* written by Josh McDowell and published by Here's Life Publishers, San Bernardino, Ca. 92414).

2. Throughout this book we have italicized certain key words and phrases, or added parenthetical material, to underscore their importance. In each instance the italics are ours. For consistency we have used the New American Standard Bible for all quotes.

3. Robert Passantino, *The Nature and Attributes of God,* Costa Mesa, Ca: CARIS, 1980, p. 3.

4. Passantino, *Nature. . . of God,* p. 10.

Chapter 2

1. C. S. Lewis. "What Are We To Make of Jesus Christ?" *The Grand Miracle: Essays from God in the Dock.* New York: Ballantine, 1983, p. 113.

2. According to Nigel Turner, who contributed the volume on syntax in the famous three-volume Moulton-Howard Turner *Grammar of the New Testament Greek,* in his *Grammatical Insights into the Greek New Testament,* Edinburgh, Scotland: T.& T. Clark, 1965, p. 15.

3. Herbert C. Leupold, *Exposition of Isaiah,* Vol. 1, Grand Rapids, MI: Baker Book House, 1968, p. 158.

4. Bruce M. Metzger, *The Jehovah's Witnesses and Jesus Christ,* Princeton, NJ: Theological Book Agency, 1953, p. 75.

5. F. F. Bruce, *Answers to Questions,* Grand Rapids: Zondervan, 1973, p. 66.

6. F. F. Bruce, *The Deity of Christ,* Manchester, England: Wright's [Sandbach] Ltd., 1964, pp. 25, 26.

7. O. P. Hogg and W. E. Vine, *The Epistles to the Thessalonians,* Fincastle, VA: Scripture Truth Book Co., 1959, p. 24.

8. Lewis, *Grand Miracle,* p. 112.

9. Lewis Sperry Chafer, *Systematic Theology,* Vol. 5, Dallas: Dallas Seminary Press, 1948, p. 23.

10. A. T. Robertson, *Word Pictures in the New Testament,* Vol. 1, Nashville, TN: Broadman Press, 1930, p. 268.

11. Robert Alan Cole, *The Gospel According to St. Mark,* Grand Rapids, MI: Erdmans, 1961, p. 67.

Chapter 3

1. The Christian view does not make all physical existence divine. In pantheism ("God is everything"), if we annihilate the creation, we annihilate part of God (unless, as Hindus say, all is illusion). Nevertheless, from the Christian perspective, God is "in" the creation in a similar (though not identical) manner in which Brahma ("world soul") is "in" the creation, according to Vedantic metaphysics (the Vedas are the Hindu sacred writings). Although there is a similarity, the differences are vital.

2. Robert Passantino, *The Nature and Attributes of God,* Costa Mesa, CA: CARIS, 1980, p. 6).

3. John F. Walvoord, *Jesus Christ Our Lord,* Chicago: Moody Press, 1969, p. 29.

4. Thomas Schultz, "The Doctrine of the Person of Christ With an Emphasis Upon the Hypostatic Union," (theological diss., Dallas Theological Seminary, 1962), pp. 194, 195.

5. Walvoord, *Jesus Christ,* p.31.

6. For a good treatement of the Old Testament appearance of God, read Volume 5 of *Systematic Theology* by Lewis Sperry Chafer (Dallas, Tex: Dallas Seminary Press, 1948), pages 31-33.

7. F.F. Bruce, *The Deity of Christ,* Manchester, England: Wright's [Sandbach] LTD., 1964, p.25.

8. G. Campbell Morgan, *The Gospel According To John,* Old Tappan, NJ: Fleming H. Revell Co., n.d., p. 161.

9. William Barclay, *The Gospel of John,* Vol. II, Philadelphia: Westminster Press, 1956, pp. 42, 43.

Chapter 4

1. C.S. Lewis, *Mere Christianity*, New York: MacMillan Publishing Co., 1943, 1960 printing, p.56.

Chapter 5

1. Leon Morris, *Studies in the Fourth Gospel*, Grand Rapids, MI: Eerdmans Publishing Co., 1969, p. 50.
2. E. W. Hengstenberg, *Commentary on The Gospel of St. John*, Minneapolis, MN: Klock and Klock Christian Publishers, 1865, p. 270.
3. C. K. Barrett, *The Gospel According to St. John*, Philadelphia, PA: Westminster Press, 1978, p. 256.
4. Joseph H. Thayer, *New Thayer Greek-English Lexicon*, Grand Rapids, MI: Zondervan Publishing House, 1977, p. 665.
5. C. S. Lewis, *Mere Christianity*, New York: MacMillan Publishing Co., 1943, pp. 65-66.
6. *Strong's Exhaustive Concordance*, Nashville, TN: Abingdon Press, 1890, p. 73.
7. Donald Guthrie, *New Testament Theology*, Downers Grove: Inter-Varsity Press, 1981, pp. 275-278.
8. Gleason L. Archer, *Encyclopedia of Bible Difficulties*, Grand Rapids, MI: Zondervan Publishing House, 1982, p. 323.
9. W.G.T. Shedd, *Dogmatic Theology*, Vol. I., 2nd Ed., New York: Scribner, 1888, pp. 312-313.
10. Thomas Schultz, "The Doctrine of the Person of Christ With an Emphasis Upon the Hypostatic Union" (theological diss., Dallas Theological Seminary, 1962), p.182.
11. Loraine Boettner, *Studies in Theology*, Grand Rapids, MI: William V. Eerdmans, 1947, pp. 152, 153.
12. Schultz, "Christ," p.181.

Chapter 6

1. Most university libraries of any size probably will have English translations of their writings for those wishing to research this topic further.

2. J. B. Lightfoot, "Epistle of Polycarp to the church at Philippi," *The Apostolic Fathers,* Part II, New York: Macmillan and Co., 1889, Vol. 2, No. 3, p. 476.

3. Edgar J. Goodspeed, *The Apostolic Fathers: An American Translation,* New York: Harper & Row, 1950, p. 85.

4. Lightfoot, *Fathers,* Vol. 2, No. 2, p. 572.

5. ibid., p. 569.

6. Kirsopp Lake, trans., *The Apostolic Fathers,* Vol. 1, Cambridge, MA: Loeb Classical Library, Harvard University Press, 1965, beginning on p. 173.

7. John Weldon, "The Deity of Christ," unpublished paper.

8. *Irenaeus,* Vol. 1, Book 4, *Ante-Nicene Christian Library: Translations of the Writings of the Fathers,* Alexander Roberts and James Donaldson, trans., Edinburgh, Scotland: T. & T. Clark, 1869.

9. For a fuller account read Philip Schaff's *History of the Christian Church,* Vol. II and III., Grand Rapids, MI: Eerdman's Pub., 1960.

10. Mark Noll, "How Much of a God is Jesus?—The Nicene Creed," *HIS,* Nov. '74, pp. 6,7.

11. A. H. Leitch, "Deity of Christ," *Zondervan Pictorial Encyclopedia of the Bible,* Vol. 2, Merrill C. Tinney, general editor, Grand Rapids, MI: Zondervan Publishing House, 1975, second ed., 1977, p. 88.

Chapter 7

1. Arthur W. Pink, *Exposition of the Gospel of John,* Vol. 3, Swengel, PA: Bible Truth Depot (I. C. Herendeen) 1945, p. 281, 282.

2. F. F. Bruce, *The Deity of Christ,* Manchester, England: Wright's [Sandbach] LTD, 1964, p. 24.

3. C. S. Lewis, *Mere Christianity,* New York: MacMillan Publishing Co., 1943, 1960 printing, p. 138.

4. Lewis Sperry Chafer, *Systematic Theology,* Volume 5, Dallas: Dallas Seminary Press, 1948, pp. 11, 12.

Chapter 8

1. C. S. Lewis, *They Stand Together: The Letters of C. S. Lewis to Arthur Greeves (1914-1963)*, Walter Hooper, ed., New York: MacMillan, 1979, p. 503.

Chapter 9

1. Josh's testimony has appeared in several of his previous books as well as this one. Parts of this account are taken from:
Evidence That Demands a Verdict, San Bernardino, CA: Here's Life Publishers, Inc., 1972, 1979, p. 104
More Than a Carpenter, Wheaton, IL: Tyndale House Publishers, Inc., 1977, pp. 25-34.
The Resurrection Factor, San Bernardino, CA: Here's Life Publishers, Inc., 1981, pp. 115-119.

Recommended Reading List

Doctrinal Treatments
Of the Deity of Christ

Baillie, D. M. *God Was in Christ.* New York, NY: Charles Scribner's Sons, 1948.

Bickersteth, Edward. *The Trinity.* Grand Rapids, MI: Kregel Publications, n.d.

Brumback, Carl. *God in Three Persons.* Cleveland, TN: Pathway Press, 1959.

Buell, Jon A., and O. Quentin Hyder. *Jesus: God, Ghost or Guru?* Grand Rapids, MI: Zondervan Publishing House, 1978.

Chemnitz, Martin. *The Two Natures in Christ.* J.A.O. Preus, trans. St. Louis, MO: Concordia Publishing House, 1971.

Demarest, Bruce A. *Jesus Christ: The God-Man.* Wheaton, IL: Victor Books, 1978.

Devries, Henri. *The Incarnate Son of God.* Harrisburg, PA: Christian Publications, Inc., 1921.

Franks, Robert S. *The Doctrine of the Trinity.* London: Gerald Duckworth and Company, Ltd., 1953.

Halverson, Richard C. *The Timelessness of Jesus Christ.* Ventura, CA: Regal Books, 1982.

Liddon, H. P. *The Divinity of Our Lord and Saviour Jesus Christ.* Minneapolis, MN: Klock and Klock Christian Publishers, 1867.

Mackintosh, H. R. *The Doctrine of the Person of Jesus Christ.* Edinburgh, Scotland: T. and T. Clark, 1912.

Marshall, I. Howard. *The Origins of New Testament Christology.* Downers Grove, IL: InterVarsity Press, 1976.

Martin, W. J. *The Deity of Christ.* Chicago, IL: Moody Press, 1964.

McDonald, H. D. *Jesus: Human and Divine.* Grand Rapids, MI: Zondervan Publishing House, 1968.

McDowell, Josh. *More Than a Carpenter.* Wheaton, IL: Tyndale House Publishers, Inc., 1977.

Passantino, Robert. *The Nature and Attributes of God.* Costa Mesa, CA: CARIS, 1980.

Robertson, A. T. *The Divinity of Christ in the Gospel of John.* Grand Rapids, MI: Baker Book House, 1916.

Walvoord, John F. *Jesus Christ Our Lord.* Chicago, IL: Moody Press, 1969.

Zodhiates, Spiros. *Was Christ God?* Grand Rapids, MI: William B. Eerdmans Publishing Company, 1966.

SCRIPTURE INDEX

LET'S STAY -IN- TOUCH!

If you have grown personally as a result of this material, we should stay in touch. You will want to continue in your Christian growth, and to help your faith become even stronger, our team is constantly developing new materials.

We are now publishing a monthly newsletter called 5 Minutes with Josh which will

1) tell you about those new materials as they become available
2) answer your tough questions
3) give creative tips on being an effective parent
4) let you know our ministry needs
5) keep you up to date on my speaking schedule (so you can pray).

If you would like to receive this publication, simply fill out the coupon below and send it in. By special arrangement 5 Minutes with Josh will come to you regularly — no charge.

Let's keep in touch!

Josh

☐ **Yes!** I want to receive the free subscription to 5 Minutes with JOSH

_____
NAME

_____
ADDRESS

_____
CITY, STATE/ZIP

SLC-2024

Mail To:
Josh McDowell
c/o 5 Minutes with Josh
Campus Crusade for Christ
Arrowhead Springs
San Bernardino, CA 92414